Dedicated to

the captain and navigator of my ship

Joan Palmer

Contents

1	The Adjutant Winked At Me	1
2	Love And Faith	45
3	Quaker Oats Ltd	57
4	Birth And Rebirths	89
5	The Norfolk Broads	123
6	Unforgettable Memories	159
7	Parting, Prozac And Prayers	179
	Hobson's Choice	197
	Epilogue	200

1

THE ADJUTANT WINKED AT ME

It was the end of November 1954 and I was due for demob. from the RAF in about two months time. I had enlisted as a regular airman at the age of seventeen and a half, six months before I would have been conscripted as a National Serviceman. With my usual inflated ideas of my own ability, I intended to become a pilot, so I was sent to RAF Hornchurch in Essex for a three day intensive medical and aptitude test. My educational qualifications were barely adequate to qualify me, but I had often fancied myself with the much-coveted white wings on my left breast. However, I was soon disillusioned when short-sightedness robbed me of the chance, although I sailed through the aptitude tests. Three trades were now open to me: RAF regiment, Cook, or RAF Police. I did not hesitate in choosing the RAF Police and, after three months training, emerged as LAC-Acting Corporal Carl Palmer, RAF Police.

I was posted to RAF Bletchley as an SP (Station Policeman). After two other UK postings, at RAF Pucklechurch and RAF Rudlow Manor, I was posted on Active Service to the 2nd Tactical Air Force in Germany at RAF Fassberg. At the time of this posting I was a thoroughly experienced policeman, so I soon fitted in to the large section at Fassberg. The duties of the job entailed a 24hr shift system and involved manning one or other of the two main guardrooms, foot patrols across the unit, or mobile patrols of the sixteen square miles of the unit which had only seven years previously been a Luftwaffe station in Hitler's Germany.

Much of the time, life was boring, but there was excitement too. Night work often involved the interception and arrest of intruders from the Russian zone who would break into our buildings and steal. Driving Land Rovers alongside the winking lights of our three main runways as our squadrons practised night flying, was always an exciting operation.

As a policeman, standards of personal cleanliness and dress were an important part of duty. Police were expected to be cleanly dressed and smart so that examples could be shown and, there-

Chapter 1 / THE ADJUTANT WINKED AT ME

fore criticism levelled at the human traffic in and out of the station. The man in charge of the guardroom was also responsible for the custody of prisoners in the cells and, obviously, for the condition of those cells. Another important responsibility was the conduct of parading defaulters. People who had been given summary punishment by the court on the station, might be sentenced to seven or fourteen days fatigues, called "jankers" by the common throng. They would parade outside the guardroom twice a day, normally at 0800 and 2100hrs, sometimes in full kit where the duty NCO would inspect them for cleanliness and neatness. Some of my colleagues were kinder than others in this procedure. One of the nastiest tricks in these inspections was to stand behind the group on parade, particularly if it included women, and make snide comments. A particularly sadistic man I knew was heard to say, in the tender ear of an unfortunate, frightened young WAAF, "Stand still then, darlin', I'm tryin' to see if your seams are straight."

The reader will understand why most ex-service men and women hated the sight of service police.

I had learned, by the time I was due for demob that extreme and intimidating tactics were unnecessary and was gratified to hear from time to time from the queue waiting to book in outside the guardroom, "It's OK. Taff Palmer's on."

However, I had also learned enough about human nature not to allow my tendency to leniency to be exploited.

There was the tough side to the police job, too, when the duty NCO had to use his powers of arrest, or break up a fight between drunks in a billet in the middle of the night.

RAF Fassberg had its own broadcasting station and soon after I arrived there I auditioned and was accepted as a regular reader, actor and, eventually producer of plays on the air.

Most importantly, I became a prominent figure in the life of the congregation at St Paul's, the camp C of E church, another step in the Christian pilgrimage which has always accompanied my life.

I have taken time to make this detailed description of the setting in which this shocking story occurs, to increase the impact of my fall from grace as a policeman, primarily, but also as a well-known and trusted member of the community. Read on, but, brace yourself!

It was the end of November 1954 and on the night in question, I was the senior of two corporal policemen. Although only twenty years old, I was the senior. My colleague whom I did not like, was a man called Brian Slater. His broad cockney accent and his oft-exhibited scorn for all things Welsh, and his sneering use of "Taff" were fast making me

Chapter 1 / THE ADJUTANT WINKED AT ME

his deadly enemy. We were on the 1600 hrs to 2359 hrs shift on this particular night patrolling the sixteen sq miles of our unit on which there were three operational runways. Two squadrons of Venom and Vampire fighter aircraft were based at Fassberg.

It was a fairly easy job we had to do. Every hour we would travel from one end of the base to the other in our khaki-camouflaged Land Rover, meeting with German dog-handlers, and signing in at checkpoints fixed at various land-marks on the huge base which had housed the Luftwaffe in the 39-45 war. As the senior, and driver of the vehicle, I made the decisions and was responsible for the patrol.

"Taff," he said, from the darkness beside me as we were driving towards the eastern gate, "I got a date with two birds from Hermansberg after this shift. Fancy coming along? Mine's a cert and she's bringing her friend tonight. How about going in the Land Rover? It is only a couple of miles from the Trauen gate." I could feel his eyes on me as I listened to the characteristic scream of the vehicle's tyres.

"Forget it Slater," I grunted. "This truck is going back to the MT at 2359".

There must have been enough strength in my voice to stop any further attempts, for there was silence, but only for a moment.

THE ADJUTANT WINKED AT ME / Carl Palmer

"Your loss, Taffy," he said, making me squirm again. He had a high-pitched chuckle as he leaned forward to smile up at me as I drove. I caught a whiff of nicotine-laden breath and hated him, for his invitation had tempted me.

I enjoyed my life in Germany. I didn't go out to neighbouring towns and villages much, as I was involved with the Forces Broadcasting service on the unit, reading short stories live most nights. I also produced radio plays and took part regularly in poetry readings with other airmen and wives and other servicemen on the station. In this way, I had become a well-known person there. I was also active as a confirmed Christian and regular communicant. I worked with the Padre and other families and servicemen to support the practice of religion commonplace on most armed service stations in the 50's.

Only a month earlier, I had attended an Ordinands' course, held for all ranks interested in becoming priests when released from the RAF. Mixing with other young men similarly minded in a secluded mansion outside Cologne had proved to be a hugely rewarding experience, after which I had decided not to go any further into such a commitment because I was too powerfully drawn to relationships with the opposite sex and the conflict with a burgeoning spirituality was too challenging.

Chapter 1 / THE ADJUTANT WINKED AT ME

Now I see that my awakening to my natural desires was to be expected at twenty years of age, but then, the "animal" in me appeared like Dr. Jekyll had to Mr. Hyde.

Here was Slater, like the local devil's agent offering me something on a plate which I knew would entail my losing an unblemished name, and my mind was inflamed at the prospect of accepting it. "They've got a nice little house on the outskirts of Hermansberg, used to be a farmhouse I think," said the devil. Your's is older than mine, used to be a teacher, I think."

The voice came out of the darkness beside me, just as we were running alongside Number Two runway, the red and yellow navigation lights on the ground either side of the runway's tarmac beside us. Part of our duty, was to look out for thieves who came over from the Russian zone on bikes to steal blankets and whatever else they could get their hands on by breaking into the Equipment section. At the end of this runway, we were due to rendezvous with one of the German Service organization dog-handlers who were hugely effective in policing the unit. There he was, a dark figure in his dark green uniform with his Alsatian "Trigger" from whom he was inseparable. I told Slater to sign his book.

"Guten abend, Corpel Palmer." he said, as he passed his duty book to Slater.

"All clear, Gunther?" I said, "Allus in ordnung," he said, giving us a smart salute, and clicking his heels which always scared me.

We moved on towards the NAAFI where we would take our evening break for a half hour before completing our shift at midnight. As we parked and locked the vehicle, Slater said, "Come on Taff. You know you fancy it. It'll be easy: we can be there and back in an hour."

"Shut it Slater. You keep on and I'll get nasty." I looked at his pock-marked cheeks under his white Police hat. "I get demobbed in January. I gotta keep my nose clean, gettit?"

I spoke harshly because two years in the service had taught me the sort of language vermin like him understood. Any reference to conscience or finer feelings would have been lost on him. We ate our beans on toast in the NAAFI in silence, though in the sorely-tempted mind of a young and "longing for experience" twenty year old, I was wrestling with my natural instincts.

"Shall I go along just for Slater's sake? Perhaps my blind date is really beautiful. Perhaps she is THE one for me."

We finished our meal and hurried back to the car because we had a checkpoint to make. I started the

Chapter 1 / THE ADJUTANT WINKED AT ME

engine, turned to Slater and said, "You will never mention this to anyone in the section, or anyone at all. Is that clear? OK, we'll go to Hermansberg when we come off at 23.59, OK?"

I think he was really shocked as he looked at me and said, "Good boy Taff. You won't regret it" He could not have been more wrong. We travelled through the Trauen gate on the east side of Fassberg at exactly two minutes past midnight. I had a distinct sense of foreboding, the hair prickled on the back of my neck as Slater, now off duty, started to chuckle to himself about the treats in store for us. Not many minutes into the future, I was to understand why he chuckled. Here I was in charge of a vehicle owned by the Air Ministry, without authorization at large in occupied Germany, on active service, with a loaded fire-arm in my holster, stealing petrol, because that was what it amounted to, with a junior NCO for whom I was responsible, an accomplice to my offences. Who were they going to throw the book at if we were caught, not Slater?

Within ten minutes we were in the outskirts of Hermansberg and I had just learned from the hideous accomplice that his girl was called Ilse and mine was called Eva. "Slow down, Taff. We're nearly there. There she is, look. The last door on the right."

THE ADJUTANT WINKED AT ME / Carl Palmer

We were in a short street of small terraced cottages, and as we approached the house he had described, a girl walked down the pathway to the house. I stopped the car and Slater jumped out.

"Hello, darlin'," he said, taking the girl in his arms and kissing her. "Taff this is Ilse - Ilse meet Taff."

The girl held out a hand to greet me. As I took her hand in mine, I could not help a smile, thrilled at her attractiveness. "Beauty", I should have said. She was quite tall with dark brown hair and eyes to match. Then she smiled at me and spoke in such a low voice, I felt myself flushing with embarrassment because it was the same tone as my girlfriend's in Wales.

"Hello, Teff. Is a funny name." she laughed aloud showing perfectly even teeth, and I was lost! She took my hand to my intense delight, I would have followed her anywhere and led me. "Come, Teff. Meet my friend, Eva." I followed her into the house past Slater, through a narrow hallway to an archway at its end into a small sitting room at the back of the house. The room was lit only by a standard lamp and was meagrely furnished with a couch and a little table beside it. "Eva," called Ilse. "This Teff," The woman at the table stood up and smiled.

Fifty three years later, I still blush and feel hot with shame at the memory. I was just twenty years

Chapter 1 / THE ADJUTANT WINKED AT ME

of age being introduced to someone more than twice my age. I still wonder whether she could have been Ilse's mother. At the time I was bitterly disappointed and furious with Slater for tricking me into meeting this poor woman. Detestable of me, I know; still, a part of me hates me because I feel strongly that looks matter. This theory makes any right-thinking person feel wretched to own as his opinion, because the inference from such an opinion is that one believes one handsome and good-looking. At that time my main concern was not to show a true reaction for Eva's sake. She must not be humiliated at any cost. I like to think it was my innate kindness that saved the situation, because in my mind, I had to admit there was no chance that I could have responded to her in love-making.

Her face, I could tell, had been good-looking in youth. Now, the tortoiseshell-framed and thick glasses and the white unhealthy-looking, flabby skin, the greyish, blonde plait she wore and the twin gold incisors bespoke the advancing years. Germany, in the fifties, was still trying to get to her feet, so clothes were hard to come by. The fading pink cardigan Eva wore, and the voluminous knitted skirt had also seen better days.

"Hello, Teff," she said, "Now, I know the British always call men from Wales, Teff. What is your real name?"

THE ADJUTANT WINKED AT ME / *Carl Palmer*

She smiled again, flashing those gold crowns at me. The effect of this was to make me flinch with the sheer lack of allure in Eva for me, but I had to press on. My mind was racing in the search for a way out.

"Carl, but spelled the English way," I said.

Ilse handed me a glass of wine, at this point. "Bob and I will leave you two alone to get known," she said. Her closeness and beauty, and the broken English made her more attractive. The obvious prearranged plan to leave me alone with Eva could only mean one thing.

Slater spoke from the door behind me, "I'll just be upstairs. Give us a shout if you need any help, Taff." I turned in time to give him such a withering look which told him if he had been closer, I would have strangled him.

When I turned back, Eva had moved to sit on a couch in the small bay window of the room.

"Come, Carl, sit next to Eva, tell me all about yourself." she smiled and patted the seat beside her. Her English was clear and fluent, and her voice was pleasingly low. I went to the couch and sat next to her. I placed my wine-glass on the adjacent coffee table and noticed she had removed her glasses. At close quarters my guess at her age was confirmed, but the perfume she wore was pleasant and I noticed her eyes were very large and bright sky blue. There was a hypnotic quality about them. I was embarrassed by the time it was taking me to reply, and I

Chapter 1 / THE ADJUTANT WINKED AT ME

could see she knew she was winning me, because her lips had formed into a smile as she sensed she was winning.

My throat was dry, I blurted, "Nothing much to tell, really. I come from a place called Cardiff. I'm 21 yrs old and I'm due for demob in January, I hope."

She was virtually hypnotizing me. She leaned forward towards me, in this low voice, she said "Twenty! You will be leaving Germany." then, I felt a warm hand high up on my thigh, as she brought her face close to mine. "You have a girl friend in Cardiff, Carl?"

I will never forget the feeling of Eva's hand on my leg. It was as though she had waved a magic wand, so that the prospect of getting closer to her seemed to be the only course open to me. Unattractive? What could I have been thinking about? She was the most sexy woman I had ever met. Her hand moved on my thigh, but her question about Joan had given me the excuse I had sought.

It wasn't strength of will; it wasn't virtue; it was simply my terror of the possibility of the RAF discovering my crime that enabled me to say," I have just become engaged to Joan in Cardiff. Eva, you don't understand. I am in charge of this patrol. If we are caught by the police, I could well end up in prison for this offence. Excuse me." I moved quickly in to the hall, shouting up the stairs, "Slater, we're leaving." There was no reply. I stood there, not

THE ADJUTANT WINKED AT ME / *Carl Palmer*

knowing what to do next. I became aware that Eva was standing behind me. She put her arms around me from the back and I felt the warmth of her body pressing into me, and the warm whispering German sounds in my ear. Her perfume started to get to me again I arched back against her.

"Don't you like me chust a liddle bit, Carl?" Her hands squeezed my midriff and lower, I knew my body must respond to her. I turned to her and held her close only just in time. I found I was looking at a family picture on the wall behind her. A tall German officer in uniform was arm in arm with Ilse on one arm and Eva on the other. The caption read "Ilse, Eva and Karl. Berlin 1943."

Eva guessing I had seen the picture stepped back from me. The beautiful eyes were cloudy with tears as she said, "Ja Carl. That is my Karl. He never came back from the Russian front." She buried her face in my chest, and I comforted her as Slater clumped down the stairs.

"Orright, Taff. You're in charge. We leaving, are we? I told Ilse we'll run her home, it's only a mile nearer the village." I nodded to him and turned to Eva, "Eva, we must get back to our unit now. Please understand." I squeezed her shoulders, and moved quickly out and to the car. Within minutes the three joined me in the car, Eva sitting next to me. I did a three-point turn and was soon facing back the way we had come. I snatched a quick look

Chapter 1 / THE ADJUTANT WINKED AT ME

at Eva who smiled at me and put her hand on my leg again. I was driving quite fast along a narrow unlit road, and, of course, on the right hand side so I had no idea what was on my left side. Ilse spoke quietly to Slater who said, "OK, Taff. Pull in here." I reluctantly stopped the car. "I'll only be a couple minutes. Just to see her to the door. That OK, Taff?" he was gone before I could answer.

The silence was a shock as I switched off the engine and sat, deeply unhappy and worried at having to wait for my detestable partner.

"I'm sorry, Eva You do understand my problem, don't you?" My voice came close to tears in this explaining and she reached and touched my face in the darkness. "There, Carl, I do understand and I am sorry you got into company with that Slater. I can see he is not a nice man"

I peered towards her in the darkness. She had said the right thing, no matter for what reason, and I leaned forward and pressed the side of her head against mine. Slater was away, heaven knows for how long and Eva's perfume was beginning to work on me. Why shouldn't I take advantage of Eva's obvious appreciation of me and do the sensible thing (Lust was beckoning and I was about to obey). I looked at her and bent to her. I was about to kiss her when a light flashed in the rear view mirror. At the same time, I heard a sound I knew well. The high-pitched roar of a VW Kombi engine coming up fast behind us. The Kombis were used extensively by the services in Germany at that time. The hair prickled on the back of my neck as the sound grew louder. The engine tone dropped as the vehicle got closer. There was a bend just in front of us, perhaps the driver was slowing because of it. No such luck. The Kombi slowed; pulled alongside us, braked sharply to a halt in front of the Land Rover and reversed towards us, and stopped. On the rear were RAF roundels and CO 61 GROUP. I was caught. Grabbing my police hat, I said to Eva, "be quiet" and unceremoniously pushed her over until she laid on the front bench seat. The driver's door of the Kombi opened and putting his hat on, Sqdn. Ldr. Torrance, CO of one of our Fighter Squadrons walked towards the car. I jumped out of the Land Rover and smartly saluted as he approached.

"Oh hello, it's you Palmer!" he said. "What are you doing here?"

Coming to attention, I saluted again and said, "Been chasing bike thieves out of the Trauen gate, Sir."

I was safe with this story, because as I have already said, thieves were a common occurrence at Fassberg.

"Ah, I see, well ....."

At this point, miles from anywhere, my luck really ran out. The sound of a woman's giggles came from Eva. With an unbelieving look, Torrance

Chapter 1 / THE ADJUTANT WINKED AT ME

pushed past me, snatched open the Land Rover's door and found Eva lying across the driving seat. "Good evening, Sir." she said.

Shutting the door, Torrance turned to me and said, "Get back to your unit at once, Palmer. You're under open arrest, understand?"

"Yes sir," I saluted.

Torrance walked back to the Kombi, slammed the door and noisily drove off.

I stood there in the darkness close to wetting my pants with fear. My worst nightmares had materialised. My mind had to accept that in a few short hours I had gone from policeman to prisoner with no one to blame but me. The most likely outcome was a Court Martial. "What will happen now, Carl?"

From the field to my right, came a cackling laugh. Slater came out of the blackness, buttoning up his battledress, incredibly scoffing, "You're in deep diffs, now Taff. Lucky I was out of the way though, wasn't it?" I just stared at him. He knew I wouldn't involve him.

"We better take Eva back to Hermansberg eh? It's not her fault is it?"

He was right. "OK, both of you, let's go then."

I decided to do a three-point turn: my mind was in a whirl. I started the engine, turning on the dipped headlights I turned the steering wheel to the left, so that we crossed to the left side of the road, then turning full lock to the right, I put the car into reverse and in complete darkness, quite quickly drove backwards to the left. There was a slight bump as the rear wheels mounted the kerb, a slight pause before the bonnet of the vehicle rose up before my eyes, and the Land Rover started to slide down a steep embankment I had not seen behind us. The car gathered speed. Eva screamed, and I braked, but we were now in a skid, as Eva screamed again. I straightened the steering wheel as we continued to career backwards until, with a sickening thud we landed in thick mud at the bottom of the slope. Desperate, I slammed the four-wheel drive in and revved. All that happened was that the wheels spun and dug us in deeper.

Now my fate was sealed. A charge of driving carelessly, thus damaging Air Ministry property, would be added to the charge list.

I broke the stunned silence, "Right, you two will have to go. Let's get out while we can." They needed no further prompting, and we all scrambled up the embankment till we arrived muddied and breathless at the roadside.

Eva said, "I will go home alone. Carl, if you give me the Fassberg number, I will tell them where you are. They will send a breakdown lorry, yes?"

"Thanks Eva," I wrote the unit number on a scrap of paper and gave it to her." Just ask for the Guardroom. They will know what to do." I touched

Chapter 1 / THE ADJUTANT WINKED AT ME

her hand peering at her in the darkness. "I am sorry it happened, Eva, You have been very kind."

She came close to me and took my hand in hers, "It will be alright, Carl. I am sorry I laughed, I will pray for you in Church on Sunday. She kissed me on the cheek and vanished into the night.

"I'd better get orf then, Taff. If I go in through the Trauen gate, no one will see me. Orright, Taff?" Not waiting for an answer, he turned and trotted away. I shudder now at the memory of that man, content to leave me to face what we both knew could mean dishonourable discharge, followed by civilian prison sentence. I stood in the silence. Suddenly, I thanked the Lord for one very necessary advantage to my solitary state. I relieved myself down the embankment loudly as I started to take stock of the depth of my disaster.

"I will pray for you in church on Sunday," Eva had said. Surrounded by darkness, I felt lonely and deeply miserable as I realized how stupid I had been.

The rain started and a calmness came with it as I accepted the need to grapple with this frighteningly complex mountain I must now face. Would the world in the person of the authorities at Fassberg understand the youthful succumbing to temptation? As an experienced police NCO, I thought not. For a police officer in a position of trust, to so seriously disregard the law was hard to forgive. I shivered with justifiable fear at my own conclusions. Boy! Was I in trouble!! My luminous watch told me it was 20 minutes to 2. My life was about to be ruined by one and a half hours misconduct.

I thought of Eva again and of how well she had come out of this incident. That blue-eyed, direct gaze she had, had left me in no doubt of her trustworthiness. She would contact Fassberg. What would Chalky White say? Unprintable, I thought. I walked up and down, stamping my feet and swinging my arms and soon became warm. What would the church say? What would the FBS Station director say? Any person who is ex-service will know how very unpopular service police are: red caps, white caps, universally hated. A copper in trouble.... Great news!

I prayed hard, and it worked. Courage came. Within half an hour of Eva's departure, a ten ton Thorneycroft truck appeared. Without a word to me, except, "Get back in your vehicle." two sergeants from the MT section fastened a steel cable on to the front of the Land Rover and, with great ease, plucked me and it up on to the road again. Telling me to get into the back of the huge lorry, one of them drove the Land Rover back to the unit. Jolted and bumped on the short trip home, gave me time to think what was likely to happen in the future. It

Chapter 1 / THE ADJUTANT WINKED AT ME

could have been a full arrest, in which case I would have been locked in the cells. I said a short prayer of thanks aloud in the back of the lorry. No one there to hear me in any case.

Jock Hunter our senior corporal was waiting for me on the guardroom steps. "You're in deep trouble, Taff," he said in his strong Glasgow accent. "Give us your pistol, I got to put it in the safe. Chalky said ye got to go straight to your billet and turn up to be charged at 0800. What happened, Taff? Ye can forget getting out in January, now, laddie." He turned on his heel and I heard him laugh to himself as he walked into the guardroom. Bad news travels fast. When I climbed the stairs, I saw my special pal, Phil Sumner, waiting to greet me. He looked really worried

"At last, and at least you're not hurt" he said "For heaven's sake, Carl!

What were you doing off the unit? Was Slater with you?"

I talked to him for about half an hour inventing a rendezvous with Eva after meeting her in a cafe in Unterluss. I gave no details of our meeting that night, but I told Phil that Slater had not been with me because I had dropped him at the Trauen gate on my way out at midnight. From the way Phil looked at me, I could tell he didn't believe me and that made me feel guilty and I decided I would tell him the truth when I was clear of the current mess. Phil could see I was just about all in, so with a strange look, he left me for the night, saying, like the friend he was, he would come to the guardroom with me in the morning to help me face the music. I soon washed and undressed and went to bed. Sleep of sorts came for a couple of hours. I rose at about 0600 hrs, shaved and sat waiting for my trip to the guardroom, pondering what the list on the charge sheet would disclose. I knew that Chalky would guess that Slater would have been the one to lead me astray, but I was determined not to implicate Slater because that would lead to additional charges as I had been the NCO ic and should have known better.

At 0750 I walked up to the guardroom to find that Sergeant "chalky" White was already in his office, at the rear of the large room. On the counter, as we called it were the "signing in and out" register and the vehicles register, but to my surprise there was Slater, large as life and twice as 'orrible. I could hardly credit the cheek of him.

"ello Taff. Who's been a naughty boy, then? Sergeant White says you're to go straight in." and the loathsome rat actually winked at me.

I ignored him. He already knew he was safe, because he had seen Chalky. I marched past his smirk and knocked on the office door.

Chapter 1 / THE ADJUTANT WINKED AT ME

"Come in" I entered, coming face to face with my boss whose expression told me the worst. He was really upset.

I was at Fassberg when Chalky had been posted to us about 18 months previously and we had always got on well, now his glowering face told me all that had changed.

"Sit down, Palmer. What the bloody hell were you playing at Taff? I was called to the Officers' mess at 0140 to explain to Sqdn. Leader Torrance, and the Station Commander what one of my most trusted police men had been doing at Hermansberg with a German bird in the front seat of one of our Land Rovers." he paused. "You haven't got a leg to stand on. They're goin' to throw the bloody book at you" he almost bellowed this.

I stood there saying nothing. The desire to go to the toilet was becoming very urgent. No sound from the sergeant for seconds.

"Now, I'll ask you this just once, tell me the truth, Taff. Was Slater with you?"

"No, Serge. I dropped him at the Trauen gate on the way out." I said.

He looked at me for an endless half minute. "Was it just a date with a bird that got you into this disaster? Cos I mean it is a disaster. They are talking about a court martial. You've kept your nose clean for the whole of your tour out here, then you throw it all away to go necking with some bird in the middle of the night without authority to be off the unit and fully armed on active service. You must be bloody mad."

I knew he wanted me to implicate Slater, but I was not going to do it.

"Right, then" He put on his hat, and said. "Stand to attention. Corporal Palmer, you are confined to camp until further orders. You will remain on permanent day shift in this guardroom. You are banned from driving any of the service vehicles. I will give you a copy of the charges framed against you by S. Ldr. Torrance as soon as I receive them from his squadron HQ. Is that understood?"

"Yes, sergeant," I shouted.

"Now, get out of my sight. Relieve Slater now".

I went back to the guardroom, where Slater was waiting for me, the other side of the counter. "I've signed the shift over to you, Taff. I'm off." he said. I saw him walking to one of the Yankee Jeeps we used for driving inside the unit, and found myself hoping he was really worried about the possibility that I might still decide to incriminate him. My mind was buzzing as I tried to collect my thoughts after the bollacking from Chalky. I noticed a letter for me lying beside our vehicle register. It was from Peter, the Flt Lt., in charge of Radio Fassberg -- "more torment" I thought. I wasn't wrong. He said he was sorry for my spot of bother, but he thought it better not to come to the studio till things were

Chapter 1 / THE ADJUTANT WINKED AT ME

cleared up. Friends in need were thin on the ground that day.

I made a vow not to let this first set-back get me down: in fact, I said a silent prayer for help. The morning drew on with no further incident until almost 11.30, then the internal phone rang.

I picked it up, "Main Guardroom," I said. "Carl, it's the padre here. When do you get off, 1600 isn't it? "

"Yes, father," I said. The tears coming to my eyes.

"Would you like to come to us for tea? I knew something was wrong when you missed communion this morning. I heard you've got a spot of bother; you'd better come and talk about it. Is that OK? "

"Yes, Sir."

"We'll see you in quarters at about 1700, Carl"

Something about silver linings went through my mind as I felt the safety net of faith underneath me once again.

The day shift dragged by. Phil came in at 1130 to ask me if I wanted him to get me a NAAFI sandwich for lunch in the guardroom to save me running the gauntlet of prying eyes if I went to the corporals' club. Of course, I thanked him and agreed. A busy afternoon of comings and going ensued on my shift. I was glad of plenty to do. My 1630 relief was on time so I was able to go to my billet and clean up before going to my tea time at the Padre's house.

I rang the bell at 1700 hrs. The man himself answered. After greeting his wife, Glenys, who gave me such a sympathetic look I was nearly unmanned, I was soon sitting in front of the Padre's desk in his office.

"Well, Carl. Do you want to talk about it? The CO rang me early this morning and asked me if I knew the policeman Jack Torrance came across with a lady in his car near Hermansberg. The CO knows you are one of our key people in St Faiths. What on earth were you thinking of?"

"Guilty as charged, Sir. Someone in the section made a blind date for me. A girl called Eva, and I met her in a cafe in Hermansberg" I looked at him. "I'm sorry, Sir. I know I've let you down."

"Who was this chap from the section? No, I mustn't ask you that. Tell me, Carl. Were you on your own last night?"

"Yes, Sir. No one is to blame but me. I took the decision to go to meet this girl, so I must accept the consequences." I looked the Padre in the eyes and he understood that I would say no more.

"Thank you, Carl. I am afraid the CO takes a serious view of this matter: you can understand why. A police officer, betrayal of trust etc., I'll have a word with him and of course offer myself as a character witness. You see, with an unblemished

Chapter 1 / THE ADJUTANT WINKED AT ME

record like yours, it was felt you must have been led astray, but you tell me that was not the case" he paused. I said nothing. "Right, we must make the best of it then" He rose from his seat and led the way into the breakfast room. With no further reference to me, we sat down with his wife and chatted until it was time for me to leave and return to my billet. As I walked briskly, I counted myself very lucky that I had such friends who would do all they could to support me. But, I also felt the burden of guilt for that betrayal of trust which the Padre had mentioned with gravity, because I couldn't forgive myself for it. Sleep was a long time coming that night.

I was still going over my uncertain future as I shaved the next morning, when I heard the clatter of an envelope dropping through the letter box in our police building. When I picked it up and saw my name on it, I knew it would contain the charge sheet from Torrance's squadron HQ. I quote:
1. Driving a vehicle (AIR MINISTRY) without due care and attention.
2. Driving a vehicle without AM authority, F658 to use it
3. Under AM173, using vehicle without authorization, is stealing the fuel used thereby.
4. Allowing a German national to travel in a service vehicle.

THE ADJUTANT WINKED AT ME / Carl Palmer

5 Travelling outside the Unit with a loaded fire-arm without permission to carry it.
6 Conduct prejudicial to the good order and discipline of the Royal Air Force.

It was a shattering blow to see it in black and white. That was my name at the top of the charge sheet. I had seen hundreds of charge sheets: for the first time I realised the impact they can have. I sat down and cried uncontrollably. All the charges were indictable, i.e., could be heard by a court martial, which had the power to discharge a serviceman with ignominy and recommend a custodial sentence in a civilian prison. I hope the reader can guess how worried I was at the prospect before me. To say it looked black in the sky ahead was putting it mildly.

Whenever I have faced a crisis in my life, time seems to move with agonising slowness. I had a good idea how long the processes of law could take, not surprisingly, I had been the other side of many such cases, but now I was the accused. Three long days ago, the skies had been cloudless until my demob only weeks away; now that had changed. The only certainties ahead were the court hearings which were threatening to not only my happiness, my freedom too.

Chapter 1 / THE ADJUTANT WINKED AT ME

I knew that the next likely stage would be a hearing before the police CO, who was the Adjutant; dependant upon that would be the next stage, a hearing before the station commander. If he decided on sending me for court martial, the court had to be convened which might take weeks. I was due for demob in just over three weeks time, and this likelihood now seemed impossible.

Halfway through my next morning's work in the guardroom, Chalky came into work and confronted me across the counter with this news. "Things are looking grim for you, Palmer. The Orderly Officer just told me they are by-passing the Adjutant, because the charges are so serious. Your case is going straight to the CO this Friday morning at 10.00hrs. He took a pace backwards, "Better take your toothbrush and towel, mate. I don't think you'll be coming back to the billet." he walked towards his office chuckling. "By the way, Slater has been posted to Wahn; what d'you think of that?" He was still chuckling as he closed his office door behind him.

Why was the sergeant laughing? Why was Slater posted? Why was the CO bypassing usual procedure and taking the case himself?
That was the easiest question to answer. Because of the time factor: there would then be time to con-

vene a court martial, so deal with my sentence before demob. Oh God, help me! What am I to do?

My imagination was working overtime. Slater had been posted because they had forced him to admit he was my accomplice, therefore a further charge would be framed against me. To save prosecuting Slater, the law was now to hold me additionally guilty.

All day I paid richly for my stupidity on Saturday night, my paranoia knew no bounds. Slater had said nothing to me since our ill-fated jaunt other than what I have already reported. He had no friends in the police section. Whenever he was off duty he always left the unit in civvies and alone, and after Saturday, I knew what he got up to. Why had Chalky been so amused, perhaps it was just because he had got rid of Slater?

Things had improved. In my life I have never displayed much patience, so that to bring a decision of my fate closer was pleasing to me. I decided to write down the pros and cons of my case. This was a lesson I had learned from my beloved father.

Any judicial system appreciates the plea of guilty from an accused person, because of the saving of time and money; I had done this on the AM form provided with the charge list.

The second factor was that mine was not a crime of violence.

Thirdly, my service record was clean, without blemish, and amongst the station police NCOs I

Chapter 1 / THE ADJUTANT WINKED AT ME

was very popular. I knew the Padre would give me a hearty endorsement for always giving hugely of my time to St Faiths, and at the thought of this began to see real glimmers of hope.

Against me were the frightening betrayal of trust and the overall seriousness of the charges. I decided not to consider the possibility of what could happen to me because of my actions. As the reader will know, I stopped short of doing the deed with Eva, but I took no credit for that and freely admitted to myself that this was due to my funking it and not a claim to virtue. I quailed at the memory of Eva's promise to pray for me as I realised that of all the people involved in this story, she came out of it best.

The time between that Monday afternoon and the trial taught me a lot about myself. My sleep pattern changed so that I would nap after my day shift, and sleep patchily at night. Exhaustively all outcomes were thought through, with the result that my pessimism became confirmed.

On the Wednesday evening, I went to the Malcolm club, where junior NCOs socialised on service stations in the fifties. I had not been since my disaster and Phil my friend thought it was time to brave it out amongst the boys. Apart from a few jibes from people like Jock Hunter our dog handler who I did not care much about, in any case, I found lots of friends who wanted to buy me a drink and assure me of their good wishes on Friday, because everyone knew I was unlikely to get a light sentence, whoever tried the case. I decided to have a few pints there because of the anaesthetic properties of German lager. At about ten thirty, I staggered home with Phil, and for the first time, managed to sleep all night.

There was a note from the Padre in my pigeon hole when I took over the day shift next morning asking me to make a special point of coming to Evensong on Thursday, as he wanted a word with me after the service. I was pleased and touched, because on Thursday I did not want to be on my own if I could help it. Loneliness might be something I had to practise in the near future.

After the shift on Thursday, Chalky wanted a word with me.

"Phil Sumner says he'll do your relief at 0945 tomorrow. I'll march you over to GHQ," He looked embarrassed. "Look, Taff, I am sorry this 'as happened to you. What ever the CO decides tomorrow, I don't want any 'ard feelings between us, right? Why you did what you did God only knows: you've been a bloody good staff copper for me, OK?" he paused for my response, which was stuck somewhere between my tear ducts and my throat. "Go on, get outta here, and bring your toothbrush and

Chapter 1 / THE ADJUTANT WINKED AT ME

a towel in the morning." This was shouted to my retreating back.

Phil and I went for tea in the mess. Some wag whistled the dead march when we got to our table, but I took no notice of him, but Phil did. "Excuse me Taff," he said.

As I have said, Phil was bigger than me, and he rose and walked over to the whistler who worked in the MT section. He leaned close to him and spoke for about a half minute in the poor man's ear. He stood and started to come back then turned quickly, "Right," he snapped, pointing a finger. His red-faced victim muttered, "Yes, Corp." pushed his plate to one side and quickly left the Mess.

"Thanks, Phil. What did you say to him?" I asked.

"Nothing much. I told him he now had an enemy in the main guardroom, ME. I think he got the point," said Phil. There is a marvellous camaraderie in service life which has no equivalent in civilian friendship.

After eating, Phil and I went to the evening service at St Faith's. There were about twenty people in the congregation, who had all greeted me as normal although they were bound to know my current problem. We were in late Advent, and suddenly I realised the joy of the Christ child was a fact in front of me, so that I was able to see the light and hope I had always found in my faith. The sincerity and warm good wishes of people who shook my hand and smiled their good will brought tears to my eyes, but gladness to my heart when the Padre approached at the end of the service. "My office for five minutes, Carl?" I told Phil I would see him later, and followed the Padre to his office.

"Sit down, Carl," he entered the details of the service into the Church log. He sat back at his desk, put his pen down, looked hard at me and said, "I have got to go to Buckberg tomorrow, so I won't be able to appear for you in the hearing." Sensing my dismay and sinking feeling, he held up his hand, "I wanted you to know I have seen the CO several times on this matter. I have given him a written testimony of your total work and ministry at Fassberg. In view of this I have also done something unusual, which I have never done before." he paused. "It is not only Glenys and me, but all your many friends on the unit prompted me to do this. I have made a plea for his clemency in view of this serious nature of the charges to be heard tomorrow." I could not find a voice, so I rose to my feet. The lump in my throat moved far enough for me to murmur, "Thank you very much, Sir." I turned towards the door and walked out.

"Oh, Carl," he called, "The Sunday sheets are in the porch. Take one on the way out."

Chapter 1 / THE ADJUTANT WINKED AT ME

"Yes, Sir G'night." I thought, dear man, but how thoughtless. What use was the Sunday programme to me? I might be in custody by then.

I rose at 0515hrs on the Friday morning, shaved, washed, and with a particularly selfish prayer for His mercy, hoped that God would be on my side. I walked over to have a full breakfast in the Mess and was delighted to find Phil there. "Hi, Carl! Ready for the fray, then," he said, smiling at me.

Fifty three years later, I remember that lovely bloke. Fair hair, tall, always clean-shaven, ruddy, healthy cheeks, white teeth and clear powder-blue eyes which looked straight at you as he spoke in that inimitable East-Anglian accent, he stands out firmly etched in my memory. I knew he had come out early to show his support. His being there made me feel warmer and confident. During breakfast, our silence was tribute to the depth of our friendship and respect for each other.

"Thought I'd find you two booghers 'ere," punching my shoulder as he passed me was my other close friend, Harry Smith from the police section. He was a typical dour Yorkshireman from Tipton, the kindest, but most thoughtful man I ever met in the RAF. He joined us as soon as he had stacked his plate from the servery. I knew that he, like Phil, was worried about me and I remember thinking at the time, "With two friends like these, you can't be such a bad bloke."

THE ADJUTANT WINKED AT ME / Carl Palmer

I got up from the table to go back to the billet. Phil looked up, "You've got a clean record, Carl Look 'em straight in the face, mate. You've got a clean record, for heavens sake, mate. They will regard it as a one-off mate, just a slip that could 'appen to any of us"

I smiled, "Thanks, mate." I walked, without looking round towards the exit." 'Ere, mate. You're a good mate, Taff. We're all rootin for you" Harry Smith punched me on the shoulder, "Yer a good lad, Carl. We're all rootin for you," he grasped my hand. Later on I had a nasty moment as Sdn Ldr Torrance came into the guardroom. He spoke quietly to Chalky, nodded to the rest of us and left.

Chalky said, "Well, Palmer, your guilty pleas will certainly count in your favour.

Let's hope they take that into consideration"

Excitedly, for the first time, I spied a glimmer of hope: would the CO have decided to deal with me today?

Phil came to the guardroom to take over at nine-thirty. Sgt. White, smart as ever in white webbing and "best blue" told me to prepare to march under escort to the HQ block. This additional humiliation made me squirm (as it was meant to) and with a pale smile at Phil, who gave me a thumbs up and mouthed, "Best of luck", I left the guardroom and waited outside on the verandah. Chalky soon joined me and screamed a huge "Atten shun," he fell in

Chapter 1 / THE ADJUTANT WINKED AT ME

behind me, said, "Smartly, now. By the right, quick march". We clattered across the verandah, then, our boots crunching in perfect unison, we marched the two hundred yards to my fate in the Admin block. Inside HQ there was a wide hall with offices off on the right at ten yard intervals. They were signed up as Admin. Senior MO, Sqdn. Commanders of each of the three Sqdns stationed at Fassberg. At the far side of the hall, facing us was an archway with a board above it on which was printed in gold letters STATION COMMANDER. Through the archway and straight ahead was the door of the CO's room labelled "Group Captain N. Livesey DSO. DFC" and to the right, another sign "Adjutant".

After knocking once, the door to the Adjutant's office was opened, and with a brief command to me to "Stand easy", Chalky disappeared inside. There was a chair against the wall but I knew better than to use it. I heard laughter coming from somewhere near, but I could not tell where. I glanced at my watch and saw that it was exactly 10.00 hrs.

At 1015 hrs the Adjutant's door opened, Sgt. White and the station warrant officer (SWO), the most senior NCO on the unit emerged and walked past me to stand side by side outside the CO's door. There was a long pause, then, as the CO followed by the adjutant came out of his office, the SWO shouted, "AHHHHHHH TEN SHUN!" I came to attention as Chalky and the SWO did and all three of us saluted the officers who returned our salutes then stopped and looked hard at me, as though I was a strange-looking object. I was terrified and felt like going to the loo again.

The whole quartet then trooped into the CO's office. Minutes turned to twenty to the accompaniment of raised voices inside. There was a long silence, and then suddenly there was Chalky, very red-faced.

"Prisoner" he bellowed, "By the right, quick march, right wheel." and in we went to the hearing. "Prisoner," Chalky screeched." Halt."

There I was, five feet in front of the CO's desk, the Adjutant standing behind and to the right of the CO. At the right hand end of the CO's desk sat the SWO with the charge sheet in front of him.

The CO nodded and the SWO in loud and most formal style read the charges against me. Why had they chosen the SWO to be the clerk of court, I began to feel faint as my shame was read publicly; it was nothing short of torture. Within a growing certainty, I sensed that the outcome was to be the worst I had expected. For a policeman to flout the rules in this way was the most serious of offences. If I had read these charges against a defendant I had charged, I would have expected the severest sentence to be handed down. As this senior NCO slowly, and with obvious relish, pronounced the

Chapter 1 / THE ADJUTANT WINKED AT ME

well-known and dreaded "conduct prejudicial to the good order and discipline of the Royal Air Force." I sensed the worst.

"Well, Palmer. What have you got to say for yourself?" The CO's voice, with its pukkha accent established my remoteness in this frightening situation, for which I had only myself to blame. What could I say?

"I was tempted by the oldest of all, Sir. It was lust, pure and simple, and when I saw her, I realised I didn't fancy her, so I bailed out."

I said nothing. Silence. "I'm very sorry, Sir."

"I should think you are," this after a lengthy pause, came from the CO." Do you realise that you stand in peril of being discharged from the Royal Air Force with ignominy for this offence? You, a trusted police man gallivanting around the German countryside, armed and with no authority to leave the unit. The most likely outcome of this morning's hearing is that you will be sent for Court Martial. Do you realise this, Palmer?"

"Yes, Sir"

"What happened that night?" the CO leaned forward in his chair. "You are a familiar figure in the guardroom, a well-known voice on Radio Fassberg, and a well-known member of the congregation at St Faiths. Did you have a mental aberration, Palmer? Was it a sort of blackout where you did not know what you were doing?"

THE ADJUTANT WINKED AT ME / Carl Palmer

A drowning man clutches at a straw after a long pause, I said, "It must have been an aberration, Sir. It was a blind date that did not work out and I really cannot explain why I did it." I looked at him and I believe he knew I could say no more." I'm just very sorry, Sir."

The CO looked at me for a long time, sighed and lowered his eyes to the file on his desk and stared at it for some time. The silence was tense, at least for me it was tense, and stretched. Suddenly, the CO made his mind up. "I'm going to adjourn this case until after lunch. The officers involved can help me to take a decision on what to do with you, Palmer." He rose from his chair. "You will wait outside." He looked hostilely at me." the court will reconvene at 1400 hrs. March him out, Sgt. White." I came to the attention, saluted, and Chalky marched me out.

"You stay here. You are not to leave HQ. Is that clear, Palmer? You can sit on that chair and wonder, OK?" As soon as Chalky disappeared towards the guardroom, I just about collapsed on the chair. I don't remember the rest of that morning, except to say it was the longest wait of my life. People were passing all the time, but it was just as though they were a part of the plot to make me feel like an outcast, because no one spoke a word to me, except Phil who came over in his lunch hour, even then, he had had to ask Chalky's permission, to bring me

Chapter 1 / THE ADJUTANT WINKED AT ME

something to eat. It was a ham sandwich. He made a sign that he was not allowed to talk to me, and when I asked if he'd wait there while I nipped to the toilet, he said, whispered, " Make it snappy, then." I needed no second bidding and was soon solitary on the chair again. Phil left without saying anything, but at least, he gave me a thumbs up sign.

Just before two, I saw Chalky marching through the hallway towards me.

"On your feet, airman." he snapped. He left me standing there as he knocked on the CO's door, then entered shutting the door noisily behind him.

I heard him talking loudly possibly to the SWO, suddenly the door opened and he came out to stand beside me at attention. I was glad that I had been to the toilet earlier as that part of my body began to prompt again. The door opened and the SWO marched smartly out to stand in front of us. "Prisoner and hescort," he shrieked. "Aaaah ten shun. Quick march, "left wheel …. right wheel. Halt."

I was standing, at attention in front of the COs desk again.

"Stand at ease!" shrieked the SWO.

There was complete silence in the room, as I awaited my fate.

Finally, the door to the inner office creaked and started to open.

"Prisoner and hescort, Aaahten, SHUN"

THE ADJUTANT WINKED AT ME / Carl Palmer

The CO and the adjutant came through the door, the CO taking his seat behind the desk and the adjutant standing slightly to his rear and on his right side.

"Palmer, you realise that the offences you are charged with could hardly be more serious. You as an NCO in charge of a police patrol were trusted to carry out your duties and then return your pistol and the vehicle, for which you had signed, to the MT section, and the station armoury. You did not do that, fully aware that you were then in breach of AM regulations.

You knew full well that the consequences of your criminal conduct would render you likely to go for court martial, the sentencing powers of which could result in your being discharged from the Royal Air Force with ignominy, I would prefer to say, disgrace. I have consulted the Squadron commanders one of whom caught you with this German woman. I have spoken with the adjutant, who knows your work with Radio Fassberg, and to the Padre who speaks highly about your work in St Faiths. However, I am keenly aware of my responsibility as Station Commander, to all the people you betrayed by the wicked disregard of the law, you a police officer displayed on Saturday night." he stopped speaking and fixed me with his gaze, which for half a minute did not flinch. So severe was it that I looked at the adjutant and incredibly, he winked at me!! With a shock of delight, I understood I was

Chapter 1 / THE ADJUTANT WINKED AT ME

about to escape! When I turned back, the CO was looking down at his papers

"In the light of your previous good conduct, and I stress this, because I have been asked to temper justice with mercy." The CO paused, "How many days to demob, Palmer?"

"Thirty two days, Sir,"

"I am sentencing you to thirty-one days loss of privileges and a severe reprimand, Corporal Palmer."

The CO stood up and left the room, followed by the adjutant. The SWO resumed his seat and I stood dumbfounded, with Chalky White standing behind me.

"You're a lucky bastard, Palmer." The SWO said, looking far from pleased. "Get back to the guard-room and out of my sight."

Chalky touched me on the shoulder and, still unbelieving, in shock, I left the room quickly.

I was elated, but dared not show it. I was not just lucky, but the subject of a miracle. I could not believe it. Fifty years later, I feel the same, amazed that I had been allowed to escape very serious punishment for what I had done. Much lobbying of the CO must have taken place to persuade him that I was worth saving, and though I could not suppress my inner happiness, I also felt shame at the weakness in my character that had so easily given in on that fateful night.

THE ADJUTANT WINKED AT ME / *Carl Palmer*

Nearly a lifetime later, I am grateful to everyone concerned in the wise administration of RAF justice to a foolish, but not an evil young man. I cannot help wondering now how many of my contemporaries were as fortunate as I. m

-----

2

LOVE AND FAITH

It is difficult to cast my mind back to the time I was fourteen for that is a journey of sixty years. I was fourteen, in form three at a grammar school, one of the lucky minority who passed the eleven plus exam, thus entitled to enter one of the half dozen grammar schools in Cardiff. I remember that I went on my first day in short trousers, blazer, school tie and cap. By the time I had reached form three, I was a veteran of the single sex education system and in long trousers, considered grown up. Grown up at fourteen, what a ridiculous idea!

In those days, pupils were expected to choose, at the end of their first year, one of three specialisms, Arts, Science or Modern. Having made the choice, one was stuck in that category until form five. With the vivid imagination I had, which has

THE ADJUTANT WINKED AT ME / *Carl Palmer*

often led me astray, I saw myself as a brain surgeon, so I chose Science. Thereafter, I consistently flopped in the Sciences and did reasonably well in the Arts, proving, beyond doubt the stupidity of choosing at such an early stage.

By form three, I had found sufficient sense to join a group of pals, to whom I stuck for the rest of my school days.

The most important driving force in my life at fourteen was a complete fascination with girls. Now confined to the rocky country of Geriatrica, I am certain that such impulses are natural, but that was no help to me then. With no understanding as to why, I was helpless at the strange desires that shook me with such frequency and intensity. It did not help that I was the only boy in my family. Three big sisters were ahead of me, and by the time their only son came along, my parents were too old to learn how the male child needs a different kind of nurture in his progress to manhood. My group of friends helped me to learn about dealing with the irresistible need to come close to girls and join the kissing and cuddling groups in back-lanes when parents allowed you to socialise after your homework was done, or choir practice was over.

I can say with complete honesty that none of my sisters, nor my parents ever told me anything about sex, so that the whole of my learning came

Chapter 2 / LOVE AND FAITH

from biology lessons (which never included human reproduction), graphic, crude and puzzlingly-upsetting drawings on lavatory doors or walls, and earth-shattering personal and practical experience. Without the close bonds of friendship, I would have been lost. I cannot ignore the influences of Chapel, the legacy of Victorian prudishness and a series of ethical codes which the grown-ups had had to adhere to at the behest of parents who had been born in a different era. All these factors had contributed towards the ridiculous situation that made life for my generation such an assault course.

I am particularly glad that the permissive age has had the huge benefit to today's younger generation in that they know at a young age, and familiarly what I learned after stumbling in virtual ignorance through a dangerous minefield of guilt and hurtful misunderstandings.

My confirmation into the Anglican religion had one enormous and immediate benefit for me. To someone who was convinced he was living a life steeped in sin, the words of absolution spoken by a priest were, to me nothing less than life-saving! In the midst of my sexual awakening, I experienced serious fear every night as I squirmed with guilt when repeating with embarrassment "forgive us our trespasses", as I knew I would be saying those same words the following night. This conflict was disturbing me so much as I imagined that "divine retribution" was sure to snuff out my life one of these nights when I wasn't looking, so I simply did not sleep.

I became very unhappy and run down so that my family knew I was ill. With peace of mind as a target, I had to adopt a life-style which would make it easier to sleep at night. Through my religious life I learned to practise more restraint, and also realised that to use the words, "I love you" in the furtherance of sexual gratification was what really compounded the "felony". This finally helped me to see the light and my conscience was no obstacle to my getting a good night's sleep.

At about this time, I met my wife for the first time. I saw Joan crossing the road at Howard Gardens on her way back to school at Cardiff High. I stopped and gazed at her, stunned by her attractiveness. She was dark-skinned with almost black hair, and walked with a strange sway, her left hip moving partly to one side which accentuated the side to side motion. She had a Cardiff High blazer on, a calf-length black skirt and a satchel hanging over her right shoulder. She turned slightly towards me as she became aware of me standing there, probably open-mouthed staring at her. As she turned, she showed brilliant white teeth in a smile, and walked on, not pausing in her stride. The incisors I noticed

Chapter 2 / LOVE AND FAITH

protruded ever so slightly. I did not move, just continued to look after her until 150 yards away, she turned into the Parade. It was the first time I had seen my wife, but as I started to breathe again and walk towards the tram stop, I knew that one day, I would ask her to marry me.

We were not to meet again for five years. I was on embarkation leave for Aden and saw her in the bar of the New Theatre in Cardiff, and quickly set out to steal her from her boyfriend as he moved off, presumably to go to the toilet. I knew him. He had been in my class in school. I had never liked him, so that gave me a greater incentive.

In an attempt to describe what I then felt for Joan Rattenbury, I must refer to the title of this piece. To say that my feelings for Joan had nothing to do with lust and sexual desire is true. Seeing her five years after our first encounter, transformed into a young woman, completely shattered my peace. Here I was about to go to the Middle East as a serviceman on active service, confronted by the most important human being in my life. I had two weeks to do something about it. I had only occasionally thought of her in the last five years. Life as a youngster is so filled with discovery that one's energies are exhausted in dealing with them, no space being left for planning and finer feelings. Out of the blue, comes this surprising encounter, which shocked me to the core, because I realised that if I did not do something now, I might risk losing her. With absolute certainty, I knew she was the girl for me as I moved through the crowd in the bar. "Hello," I said, "Will you come out with me? My name is Carl Palmer."

"I know," she said." I've seen you at parish socials." she smiled standing two feet away from me. I was dazzled at her beauty.
"Will you come out with me?" I repeated.
"But you see, I am going out with Peter," she said with raised eyebrows, and followed it with a laugh.
"I don't care. I just want to take you out." I said. "Where d'you work? Can I ring you?"
"Lloyds Bank Whitchurch." Out of the corner of my eye, I saw Rendell returning.
"Can I ring?" I made to move away. She stepped towards me and touched my arm. "Yes, of course you can."
She must have seen the colour come into my face as I turned away, aware of my thumping heart.
I went over and over that interview, savouring that touch on my arm in the sleepless night ahead of me thinking of how soon I could see that face again.

I knew that this must be falling in love. For the first time with any woman, the excitement of seeing

Chapter 2 / LOVE AND FAITH

her again had nothing to do with sexual attraction; Joan caused a deeper sort of anticipation in me, but I was frightened that she would not think me good enough for her. It was nothing to do with stealing her away from my ex-schoolmate. That was a plus. I knew nothing of Joan's background except that she worked in a bank. In those days, banks were only open to school leavers who had done very well in their school certificates. Women candidates found it difficult even to get to the interview stage. From this fact, it was only a short step to realise that Joan must have excelled at her school cert. How would she feel going out with a boy who barely scraped the school cert? This made me feel an unworthy suitor from the start.

No matter, the next morning I rang Lloyds Bank at about ten am to be told, "Miss Rattenbury is too busy to come to the 'phone, I'm sorry". Not slightly daunted, because she might have arranged the refusal; I prayed she had not; I rang at lunchtime and was rewarded.

"Lloyds Bank, Joan Rattenbury speaking."

Had she been waiting for my call? "Hello, it's Carl."

"Hello, please don't ever ring at mid-morning, it's our busiest time," she paused and I could feel my face reddening, my blood pumping so loudly she must hear it.

"I'm sorry I couldn't speak to you."

THE ADJUTANT WINKED AT ME / Carl Palmer

I almost cried with gratitude at the reprieve. Her voice on the phone was almost deeper than I remembered.

"I'm really sorry, Joan. I won't do it again. You see I'm on embarkation leave for Aden, and I've only got a fortnight's leave left" I said.

"Please don't apologise. Gosh you do lead an exciting life." she replied. Then, as if to make up for telling me off, she took the lead.

"Do you want to take me out, then? I could see you on Friday evening if you like."

I could hardly believe it. "Yes, of course, I want us to go out. What about the wine bar in the Wyndham Arcade? Shall I meet you there at about seven?" I said.

There was a pause as though she had put her hand over the phone.

That throaty voice again, "I'll be there, Carl. Thanks for asking me. I've got to go now. We're not supposed to use the phone. Goodbye"

There was a click. She was gone. I stood there looking at the phone smiling and smiling. My life had changed at that moment, I could not have been happier. I peered into the little mirror in the kiosk, grinning wildly at myself.

That first date settled things for me. We did not hold hands. Such close intimacies arrived weeks later in those days. We talked, exploring each others histories thus far. We were only eighteen years old.

Chapter 2 / LOVE AND FAITH

Date followed date in those precious days before I left the country. The posting, delayed for another wonderful week, was changed to Buckeburg, Germany in the 2nd Tactical Air Force. I was glad not to be travelling too far from Joan, because, even then, I knew she was the woman I had to marry.

She went to a church in the same parish as me and before we parted in the autumn of 1953, we went to church together at St James the Great in Newport Road. In a mysterious way, that seemed to seal the bond between us. Both of us had a commitment to the Christian faith and, as the time came for our last evening together. I felt that fate was moving us towards a partnership for life.

In those first few weeks I had come to know her closely. An only child of working class parents, the strong element in her character fed her determination to better herself as a bank clerk. Her school results as I had guessed were far superior to mine; she should have studied further and gone to university education, but was not allowed to do so. This fact engaged my sympathy for her – so obviously deprived at 16years of age. She was also involved in amateur drama, my most burning interest, so that gave us plays to think and talk about and I knew her looks and sexy speaking voice would soon get her parts in public productions in Cardiff.

THE ADJUTANT WINKED AT ME / Carl Palmer

She was a much stronger character than I, and this feature also was influential in drawing me to her. She had most beautiful large eyes and an unnerving gaze that made me feel she could see into my mind, but the most winning characteristic was the simple trustworthiness of her, something I placed high on the list of essential qualities in a person.

As the leave petered out, I began to wish I was not leaving her. The fact that I was going to an "active service" area in Germany further added to my worries about the future.

Our last night was to be spent in Bindles in Cold Knap, near Barry. We were going to dine and dance there. I was not much of a dancer, but I could manage the waltz and the quick step without too much damage to my partner's feet.

It was a cold evening and everything went well, with an awareness in both of us that it had to, because the sadness of parting was close, and I was to leave on active service, so emotional tension threatened the evening. I had bought her a going-away present, a silver bangle which had cost a lot of money. I remember, it was £12, for 1953 a huge price. It was in an expensive case and when she opened it, her large eyes sparkled with surprise and delight. She thanked me so extravagantly, I was

Chapter 2 / LOVE AND FAITH

embarrassed and realised that she had never been given such a costly gift. My heart went out to her and I resolved to repeat the generosity as soon as I could get a leave from Germany.

We walked outside to look at the sea before travelling back to Cardiff. The moon was shining on the sea as the tide was high on Cold Knap beach. It could not have been a more romantic setting. The music from the ballroom played behind us as we stood together, a crooner with a Bing Crosby baritone was singing "It had to be you; it had to be you..."

I felt her arm creep around my waist as I put mine around her shoulders. She shivered at my touch and I quickly withdrew my arm, scared I had offended her. She moved to stand facing me, looked up into my eyes and said, "No, Carl. Hold me." She put her arms around my middle as I drew her to me, bent my head and kissed her full on the lips. How long we stood like that I will never know, but I remember the world and the night and the cold went away and I felt safe and a rightness I had not known before. It was our first kiss. We were nineteen years old. She smelled of toothpaste and had a personal fragrance enhanced by the subtle perfume that she wore, and she had opened her eyes to look into mine at the end of that kiss which left me breathless with love for her.

She smiled as we exchanged a chaste kiss goodbye at her doorstep later, because she knew I would always love her: so did I!

3

QUAKER OATS LTD

I was released from RAF service in February 1955, and after a boring time as a trainee manager with a toy retailer, I applied for the post of representative with Quaker Oats Ltd of Southall Middlesex. The territory was Swansea and the west. The most attractive feature of the job was that a car went with it and the salary was a huge £750 and expenses.

I was interviewed by a Mr. Smith area manager of Wales and the West Country, and the area coordinator who would be working closely with me. At the end of the session I was chosen amongst many candidates, to go to the Dorchester Hotel for a three day training course. All expenses would be paid and at the end of the London stay I was to travel to Southall to collect my new Ford Popular.

THE ADJUTANT WINKED AT ME / Carl Palmer

As the reader can imagine, I felt very pleased with myself.

Even then, I had serious misgivings. Swansea and the towns west of it was, and still is largely Welsh speaking, which I had mentioned at my interview, but they had both ignored it. To my shame, I was and am still a monoglot. I am intensely proud of my Welshness, but I had lived in Wales for long enough to learn that people who lived in Cardiff were no better than "the bloody English" to native Welsh speakers. They however must have been so impressed with my potential that they expected me to be able to ride above such small difficulties. I was not so sure, but to have my own car, I would give it a whirl.

The Dorchester is five star category in the West End of London, but in 1955 it was near to new and a very classy place to stay for a young and still pimply 21 year old; I was apprehensive. I need not have worried. The men attending the training conference were a new bunch of recruits to the sales force. Altogether, we were thirty in number from all over Britain. The accents and table manners at our first dinner together on that Wednesday evening betrayed the fact that class was no barrier to joining the American owned company Quaker Oats.

Chapter 3 / QUAKER OATS LTD

We had a delicious meal with suitable wines and brandy and cigars after the cheese course. I remember grimacing with embarrassment as my table neighbour grabbed three cigars before he passed the box to me. I noticed how many of my companions had to extinguish their cigars before the Loyal toast. There was no formal training that night. Area managers and coordinators moved among us giving out the training programme for Thursday and Friday and warning everybody that the conference ended officially on Saturday after breakfast. The grand commissioning dinner for all of us, was timed for 7.00pm-7.30pm on Friday evening.

Whenever I have mentioned to people that my first rep's job was for Quaker Oats, they have smiled and said, "Well, you wouldn't have much trouble selling porridge, would you?" They do not realise that Quaker also make other cereals - Puffed Wheat, Sugar Puffs, Pearl Barley, Macaroni Cheese and many more. The point is that volume selling was every big company's aim, and we were due to be indoctrinated or imbued in the Quaker way. In the fifties high pressure selling was all the rage in this country. By whatever possible means, wholesale and retail outlets were bombarded to "sell our product".

There was a strange, almost religious atmosphere amongst the staff members looking after us in that training conference. They all looked the same; the same fixed smile, short haircut, shiny mohair suit silvery-blue in colour, startlingly white shirts with cutaway collars and highly polished black shoes. The awed way in which the product was mentioned, gave me the creeps! The senior staff members all wore the blue and yellow Quaker tie, dark blue suits, and spoke loudly in strong American accents. They were all addressed as "Mr." by the English Quaker employees who spoke to their American superiors in nothing less than reverential tones.

Thursday morning found us all in the conference hall after a huge fried breakfast, for a prompt 0900hrs start. The UK Managing director introduced himself. Let's call him Thomas P Bigwood. He needed no microphone. He weighed in at about 250lbs, was forty five years old, with pink healthy cheeks, shiny prominent chin and the hardest blue eyes I had ever seen. He terrified me. The Quaker tie contrasted too much with his deacons grey suit. What shocked me most was the voice when he started his speech because it was so unexpectedly high for such a big man.

In the tones of the tenor range, with the accents of Salt Lake City, he gave us a brief history of the company, investing his words with the reverence that was beginning to annoy, rather than amuse me. He ended this section with a caution to us all,

Chapter 3 / QUAKER OATS LTD

in that we should consider ourselves fortunate, so privileged to be thought suitable to work for Quaker.

"We're gonna trust oll uv u neverrr to beetray thet trust", he fetched the table surface a crushing blow with his clenched fist and we all of us listened a lot harder. "This praduct is a wunderrful praduct and I want you guys to feel that in yerr hearrrts as ya go forth to all parts of this country for Quaker Oats". He almost sang the name. "Like me, like oll my colleagues who will soon be showing you how to work in the sales field, I want you to be proud of our praduct; it's a good praduct, not just because I say so, because the lab. says so. It's the best cereal of any cereal on sale in any of the yoor opeen countries. Ya gotta believe that."

Here he paused and looked round. Such was the loudness of his voice and threat in his gaze that no one moved or looked even slightly inattentive. Withdrawing from his pocket a huge Quaker handkerchief he slowly wiped his forehead, caught a few tears from his eyes and said. "Because we are right behind you, gennamen. You have bin picked from hundreds of people to come to work for us, and you were the best of them." For at least fifteen seconds, he looked at every table to see if there was any one who wished to argue with his claim. No one moved. "You are the best we could find and I can see that noone here is going to let us down, because you are going to deal with the best praduct on the market". He held up his hands in a silent gesture, and ever so slowly sat down.

The colleague next to him stood up and looking towards Big Tom as we later realised, smiled wagged his head in silent but reverential approval and began the applause, which quickly expanded in volume until we were all on our feet clapping and cheering as though our lives depended on it.

The next speaker dwarfed by Tom in stature and every other sense, spoke in an accent common to us all. He was a midlander and introduced us to the sample case. "At the end of this morning session, you will all be given one of these. They're made of pure English leather, with brass fittings, as you can see; expensive and smart, but inside is the secret of your success. It contains a sample of each of our products, plus advertising information, technical information on our products, and your own, up to date press and TV file". As he spoke, he had been demonstrating the contents of the case.

We then heard the sales patter, to give it its proper title, "the planned presentation". Pausing at this stage he emphasised, that the wording of this presentation had to be learned and never be deviated from. Here, I doubted for the first time.

Chapter 3 / QUAKER OATS LTD

I conjured up a picture of myself in front of a bilingual elderly grocer in Carmarthen doing the planned presentation. I was quite certain I would not be given a hearing.

The main theme of the PP as we came to know it, was to suggest to the customer-"This is the time of year when people change their breakfast habits from hot(cold) cereals to cold(hot) (dependent upon the time of year). If you give me a stock order now I can give you 20% off the wholesale price .... that is if you order more than forty cases". It seemed to me, having some idea of the Welsh response to attempts to be dictated to by some cheeky kid from Cardiff, that a punch on the nose would frequently result from such an approach.

The number of popular breakfast cereals on the market was high to put it mildly. I came to the conclusion there and then, that such tactics in Wales would fail. I never subsequently changed my mind. With the innocence and burning ambition of youth (notice. no young women) we were pleased with the simplicity of the task ahead. What more natural than a specific time of the year when people should change their breakfast habits. The army of hard-headed retailers between us and the success of the 'planned presentation' were not considered. The famous black folder in the sample case carried examples of Quaker's press campaign --- national dailies, provincial papers, cinema advertising, and the new wonder in adverts, TV commercials were all time and date listed. Quaker's latest gimmick; the Sugar Puff train was touring all the big towns in the country--dates listed. It was obvious no expense had been spared in backing up the sales force: one could not help but be impressed. In truth, we were all excited to try our hands in working with such a comprehensive scheme.

The other important angle of this conference was to teach us about the point of sale display. To link up with the advertising campaign, special card board stands should be placed on the counters of shops to offer the product being advertised. Vividly coloured, so that the memory clicked in recognition, having seen the TV ad would induce a purchase at point of sale. The stands could quickly assembled given space in the shop, and the shop owners permission, with Stanley knife (included in the sampler case). The whole scheme seemed foolproof.

Tired, but with the thought of being only days away from picking up my new car on the weekend, I went to bed, still enthused at the idea of persuading the burghers of West Wales to see the light of the Quaker method. I went to sleep dreaming of fat, shiny-suited men whispering "ya gotta blieve it! This is the finest pradduct on earth."

Chapter 3 / QUAKER OATS LTD

Friday was mostly tiresome admin. We were also told, "Remember! Your approach to wholesalers has to be entirely different. They are not concerned with press and TV campaigns; their interest is solely profit margins" (this last point said sneeringly, as though Quaker was above such trivial concerns). More talk of expense forms, of keeping your vehicle clean. Here, a private laugh at the American pronunciation of vehicle, "veehickle." Remember gennamen! Your personal appearance is of great importance. The dark suit will always have a good influence on your customer. A white shirt and shiny shoes show that you care about cleanliness; the customer will be impressed. You are there to represent Quaker Oats one of the finest companies in the market." The repetition of superlatives was beginning to set my teeth on edge.

The commissioning and farewell dinner were due to begin at 630 pm on Friday evening, so we were told at 330pm we should make our selves scarce until assembling in the hotel at 6.25 for a prompt start to the dinner. I had a snooze in my room, then listened to the radio until it was time to wash, shave and dress for dinner. At exactly half past six, I went down to the restaurant outside which most of my colleagues were waiting. The doors were firmly closed, policed by one of the senior staff. Sounds of activity could be heard inside the room, and within seconds, the double doors were flung open to reveal the brightly lit almost unrecognizable interior.

It was a long, large room with tables set out on three sides of a rectangle. The short side of the three faced us on entering the door, so that the others were lined down either side of the room.. At the far end of the room was a huge display, wide at its base, then tapering to its pinnacle at 12 ft in height. All Quaker's products were there with Quaker Oats in the centre top, flanked by Puffed Wheat on its right and Sugar Puffs on its left.

I could not help seeing it as a likeness of an altar, which is what it was intended to be, with the powerful spotlights making the whole structure gleam. At the back of my mind, I could not suppress a sense of revulsion at this worship of what was breakfast food. I felt guilty at being part of something of which I was ashamed. It made a strong impression on us all. The staff standing around and watching our reaction were pleased as from a stunned silence and led by the senior sales managers of the future, we started, slowly at first, then thunderously to applaud then to cheer our hosts among whom I spotted Big Tom.

Between the two side tables, were sample cases arranged in stacks. Large cartons with product names on their sides, a long table containing

Chapter 3 / QUAKER OATS LTD

our order books and advert files and two stanley knives for each salesman plus a huge roll of selotape. This equipment was to be used in point of sale displays.

The delighted smiles on the faces of our hosts obviously resulted from our spontaneous approval at the splendour of the highlight of their show; the brightly-lit, gleaming product display. "Gentlemen, be seated, please." boomed Thomas P. Bigwood. We did as we were bidden, and the five course banquet began. Looking back nearly fifty years to that scene, I remember how silly I felt at being part of that crazy attempt to indoctrinate us, but I also remember seeing few signs of disillusionment or sarcasm among my fellow trainees.

One or two lesser lights made short speeches to jog our memories about the planned presentation and the desperate need to put up as many as possible POS displays and the need for prompt everynight posting of order forms to Head Office. The main speech was bound to come from Big Tom, I reasoned. He would have prepared a real show stopper. I was not to be disappointed, as I noticed the party of waiters suddenly bustle about the top table. The great man, I noticed was drinking water, whilst some of his top table colleagues were swigging wine quite lustily. I had been told on the Thursday that he was a Quaker, and as I watched him I saw him casting disapproving glances at his near neighbours as they chatted noisily beside him. How could they not be aware of his obvious crossness! Suddenly he reached forward, picked up the gavel in front of his plate and brought it down twice in quick succession on the table in front of him. The effect was electrifying. It was as though all the Quaker staff were galvanised in the same second. As one they stopped talking and whatever they were doing and looked at him. There was a five second freeze, then a huge smile broke across Tom's face as he stood up.

In this strange high-pitched voice he began, quite quietly at first to talk to us in the strong American accent. Most of the trainees there were almost anaesthetised by food, wine, brandy and cigars, but such was the man's magnetism, we were soon listening intently. There was an honest glow of goodness about him. Gazing towards the huge Quaker altar of goodies, he said how honoured he felt to be commissioning another band of brothers to go forth into the land to show the good folk of this country the blessing awaiting them when they started eating Quaker food. Here there was a long pause, during which he smiled at all around as though he was seeking inspiration when in truth he was probably making sure all his colleagues were awake as he was about to ascend to the climax of his speech.

Chapter 3 / QUAKER OATS LTD

"You must see, gennamen, the importance of your mission! I have worked for this fine company all my life. It's an all-American company, but I'm proud to tell you, my family forbears (he said four bears as two words) were aboard 'The Mayflower'," and I found myself wondering whether the Sugar Puff bear had had strong links with the UK. Their home was in Southall and that is why our company built its headquarters there." At this point all the staff applauded loudly.

"I used to be in the sales force y'know, the very same sales force you lucky folks are about to join, but two years ago I moved to Wisconsin back in the Yew nited states where my lovely wife and our six boys are living now. It was the proudest moment of my life when I was made an Executive Vice President of this company!" Here he thumped the table very hard, causing the cutlery to jump and arousing one of the top table team to wake with an involuntary cry of alarm. I hoped no one else saw this as I saw his face redden with embarrassment.

"Now, gennamen," Tom was only slightly ruffled (by his colleague's huge and probably fatal gaff), "I want you to know, each and everyone of you that I care for you all as personal friends. If there is any way I can help you in your work, call me. I will be there for you". Here, the enormously effective smile then, the brushing of a tear from his eye "God bless you in your work for Quaker Oats". There was real emotion in his voice, as he took out his Quaker handkerchief, mopped his brow and eyes, waved at us and sat down as thunderous applause testified to the success of his speech.

Dazed, slightly drunk, but almost tearful at the emotion of Tom's speech, we all started to leave the banqueting room as the lights were switched off and staff members became occupied with dismantling the display and packing the equipment and merchandising and the products. As I left I glimpsed Tom Bigwood in earnest conversation with the top table colleague whose slumbers his speech had disturbed. Their body language told its own story!

Six months later, living in digs in Swansea, I came to the conclusion that I did not have the strength of will and unscrupulous attitude that were at the heart of rep's work. The planned presentation had long since ceased as part of my attempts to sell at retail and wholesale level. The scorn, rude remarks and dismissals as nonsense by the trade had won the day, and I was finding it hard to make friendly connections because of my inability to speak Welsh, my youth and because my predecessor was a local boy who now was the local rep for Kellogs. My area extended from Swansea to Pembrokeshire and north as far as Aberdyfi. This was beautiful Welsh countryside and a great pleasure to explore,

Chapter 3 / QUAKER OATS LTD

but the customers were unimpressed by my promises of advertising campaigns and product support systems, because of their rural environment in its old-fashioned way of trading. Points of sale displays were strongly resisted. My inability to speak Welsh clinched their resistance to my attempts to befriend them and I realised I was not going to stay with Quaker much longer.

There was one afternoon when, sick at heart at having done no business all morning, not even one POS display in the town which was known as the travellers graveyard, Llanelly, I sneaked my car into the car park behind the Odeon cinema, far from public gaze (as I thought) and bought myself a posh seat (one and nine pence) in the circle, to see "Captains Paradise" with Alec Guiness and Yvonne de Carlo. The huge cinema was deserted as I sat upstairs in splendid isolation, chewing a Mars bar. About halfway through, a well-known voice said from behind me. "Good film isn't it, Carl?"

It was the area manager, Mr. Smith.

Of course we left the cinema at once and found a cafe and chatted. He was very decent about it; knew all about the "travellers graveyard". When we left, it was on the understanding that my job was still safe, but he would arrange for me to be more closely supervised. The writing was on the wall!

THE ADJUTANT WINKED AT ME / *Carl Palmer*

At this time, I was well established in Swansea Little Theatre. In fact I had been cast in the lead of their next production, "Beauty and the Beast", and was well rehearsed; the production date was about three weeks away from the Odeon incident. We were to perform in the Palace Theatre in Swansea for a weeks run and were rehearsing three times a week. My close supervision continued with frequent visits from Lowry the coordinator at my side insisting that I adhered to the planned presentation every time with the same poor sales results on a regular basis. In the week before the show, I had a message from Lowry to tell me that he would meet me the following Monday morning outside D J Williams in Bridgend. This wholesaler was a fearsome character upon whom I had never made the slightest impression. He would stand and sneer at whatever I said, with a reply exactly the same on every occasion. "Nothing today, young man" turning his back on me to carry on with his poring over the ledger. I sensed that it was no accident that Lowry had picked D J Williams; he anticipated this would be my breaking point.

The weekend was filled with the excitement of intensive rehearsals both dress and technical, with the big dress rehearsal timed for seven o clock on Sunday night. Dead tired, but very excited, I left the theatre at half past midnight, contemplating the morning's interview in Bridgend.

Chapter 3 / QUAKER OATS LTD

On the way to Bridgend on Monday, I was practising my lines to D J Williams. I was not dreading the outcome because all that mattered to me was to happen when the curtain went up that evening at The Palace. Lowry's car was outside the warehouse when I arrived, so I quickly parked behind it and joined him in his big, impressive Austin Westminster.

"Now I must warn you ..." I began.

"It's all right. I have met Mr Williams before, Carl I know he is a hard nut to crack." he paused. "You can do it if you want to Carl" he splayed his hands in an explanatory gesture, and I understood the hidden agenda. "Planned presentation, mind". I walked back to my car to pick up my case, smiled at Lowry, and we walked together to the open, huge doors of D J's kingdom. I remember thinking of the gunfight at the OK corral!! Through the open doors we made our way towards the ill-lit, topless office in the middle of high stacks of cartons either side of aisles. I distinctly remember the high stack of Scotts Porage Oats leaning against the office wall.. I could see the gleaming, bald head of the stocky figure in his long brown overall which I knew to be the owner. Tapping on the closed door and gently pushing it open, I perceived the livid face of DJ.

"Good morning Mr. Williams." I paused in the glare of his hostility, but he said nothing.

"Palmer, Mr. Williams, Quaker Oats" still nothing.

With a quiet, humourless snort, I launched myself.

"This is the time of year when people change their breakfast habits from cold cereals to hot cereals. In November there is nothing more welcoming than a bowl of nutricious Quaker Oats." I looked at his glowering face, still nothing was said. "If you give me your winter order now, Sir, I can give you a 30% reduction. Can we do business?"

"Have you finished? Is that all?" said D.J.

"Yes Sir. Except to tell you..." I began

"Tell me what? What do you think you can tell me about my business? Bugger off out of it, and stop wasting my time." he turned his back and bent over the ledger on his desk. I turned to look at Lowry who had been standing behind me during the interview. He smiled thinly, and shrugged his shoulders. I picked up my sample case, said "Thank you, Mr. Williams" then pushing past my colleague, walked out of the office.

When we had returned to the car, Lowry said to me. "You know where we went wrong, I shouldn't have come in with you." he smiled and said "Now, go in on your own and I bet you'll make a sale." At this point, he had the grace to blush, for he knew

Chapter 3 / QUAKER OATS LTD

what my reply would be. For a moment I was struck dumb, until I realised he had done this before.

"Any hope of making a customer of that creature would be lost if I did what you want me to do, Mr. Lowry."

He said nothing, just kept his eyes on the pavement. "OK Mr. Lowry, I resign."

A couple of hours later, I had handed over my sample case and documentation; the car was parked in the Mackworth Hotel garage, officially returned to my employer, and Lowry and I were having a coffee and severance chat, during which it was agreed that I was not cut out for selling the Quaker way. In exchange for gamely falling on my sword, Lowry agreed to give me a month's salary in lieu of notice. As I watched his big Austin Westminster disappear on the Cardiff road, I felt nothing but relief, ahead was a week's performance as an actor! I could not have been happier.

"Quaker" was not my only failure as a salesman, or "rep", a term everyone over the age of 50 will recognise. I know now and knew then, that the reason for my failure to succeed as a salesman was a complete lack of motivation. Neither did I have the unscrupulous attitude to getting the product onto the shelves at all costs that I had seen in the nature of the champion salesmen I had known. On top of all this was the casual way in which I approached the work; i.e., I wasn't really interested. What I saw as my ideal was to work at something which, at end of a day's toil would give me the satisfaction of having helped humanity in some way. To have a sales order book was far from filling the bill.

You might have thought that I had realised from the Quaker experience I had learned my lesson, but, you see, the only way I could have my own car was to have a firm's car. Consequently, a Hillman Husky plus £800 pa went with a reps job in the "sales and promotion" of Lifeguard toilet rolls for Cardiff and the Rhondda valley, and Carl Palmer was the successful applicant. You can imagine the sales pitch for the comparative merits of bottom cleansers!

After barely three months of trying this dirty work against huge competition, I was squeezed into a corner of a tiny grocers shop in Caerphilly, my Stanley knife at the ready, constructing a point of sale display on a crowded counter of shiny red toilet rolls, when a large-breasted schoolgirl crashed into me from behind, not only demolishing my display, but causing me to almost amputate my left thumb. What I said to that hapless young lady must remain a secret, but as I waited for the grocer's wife to bandage my thumb, I realised that God was trying to tell me something about me and selling. By the end of that working day I had not only sent

Chapter 3 / QUAKER OATS LTD

off an empty order book, but also a resignation to Lifeguard Limited.

At this point, I must digress to explain that the courtship of Joan Rattenbury continued throughout all my attempts at "reps" work. Needless to say, she was becoming fed up with my wandering from job to job.

At a Christmas party following my resignation from Lifeguard, I had a minor fling with a young lady. Within days, Joan heard about it and a tempestuous scene of wiping the floor with me, told me we were finished. Who could blame her?

Christmas however, I came to my senses and gave hot pursuit.

Christmas '56 was a sad time for me, not only had I lost Joan, but I was out of work and finding it difficult to get a job. This did not prevent me from sending flowers to Joan at least twice a week and at Christmas time, I sent her all the presents I had already bought for her.

Just after Christmas I heard from one of the firms to whom I had applied offering me the post Clerk in the Advertising department. I rang them up and was told I could start work immediately, so on Monday 3rd January I started as a Small- Ads. pricer with Western Mail of Cardiff. Much encouraged by this, I decided to take a bold approach with Joan and give her an ultimatum.

THE ADJUTANT WINKED AT ME / *Carl Palmer*

We had close friends in a newly married couple who were members, like us of Everyman Theatre. I rang them up on the evening I started my new job and asked them to be go-betweens in getting Joan to forgive me. I told them I had written to Joan with my "marry me now" plan and they agreed to help me. I heard from them the following day, telling me that Joan was coming to dinner that day and she had agreed to speak to me if I phoned at about eight in the evening.

To cut a long story short, after two evenings of persuasion, we met on the third evening, just the two of us, and Joan agreed to marry me on Saturday the 19th January in the Registry Office in Cardiff. I know Joan married me partly to escape from her parents, but mainly because she loved me. (That's my story and I'm sticking to it!) By special licence, Joan married me on that Saturday morning in front of our parents and a select few friends, adjourning to the New Continental restaurant for the luncheon which was paid for by my father-in-law at a cost of £8 including drinks.

I smile and feel good at the memory. It was the best move I had made in my life to date. We had a swift honeymoon in a swish West End hotel, thanks to my father's £50 and I knew my life would take sensible shape thereafter. The strength that I had

Chapter 3 / QUAKER OATS LTD

spotted in Joan years earlier was something of a daily presence and it was that in its exemplary effect. There it made something of me, but not in the immediate future. An early maturity is something of which I can never boast. Fortunately, my new wife was as much interested in theatre as I was. Whenever there was a new production on the stocks, everything else in our life together took second place. This was a good thing in many ways, because it was to point to my means of earning a living, eventually, but there were still a few wrong turnings that I was doomed to take which caused severe trials to marital harmony.

For almost the first year in wedlock, I continued with the Western Mail. It was a basic clerical job with no means of promotion, so Joan often hinted that I should be looking for a job with prospects. By December of '56 I had found something far more promising in the personnel department of the Central Electricity Generating Board. My father was pleased about this as he was still a senior accountant in an allied concern. He bought me books on accountancy and suggested that I studied to become a chartered secretary; I bridled, this sounded far too serious for me, but I became involved in the social side of staff welfare and, if I had showed "stickability" I might have done well, however something exciting happened. In the autumn of 1958, contrary to the general opinion, I proved I was a man, when my beloved wife announced that our first child was on the way. I was elated! With hindsight, I realise that this was what, in the long run would prove that I was soon to move in the right direction.

For the moment, more mistakes to be made. The first mistake was to create near catastrophe! I thought that the most sensible thing to obtain was a car in which to carry my new baby around, so not telling Joan, I threw almost eighteen months of creditable efforts in the CEGB in the bin and got a rep's job selling evaporated milk in the Rhondda valley.

This new job was to make selling fridges to Eskimos a matter of child's play. Let me explain. The world-wide, famous Nestle had, for many years been supplying a product called Ideal milk. Throughout my childhood in South Wales I had been familiar with this product as it was a Sunday afternoon treat to be spread on the tinned fruit we always had for tea. Consequently I expected resistance when I tried to change the minds of grocers in my territory in the Rhondda. Our product was just as good, they told us in the training conference. It was called "Carnation milk", and was contained in a bright red can. Nestle, Ideal milk was so well established that I was completely unable to sell Carnation anywhere on my territory.

Chapter 3 / QUAKER OATS LTD

It was simply the power of advertising that had bonded the two words "Ideal" and "Milk" in the minds of everyone I met. You see, it was not Ideal evaporated milk that was my competitor, but, a new product, "Ideelmilk". I knew the battle could never be won.

Joan's pregnancy proceeded without any trouble and in my eyes she grew daily more beautiful as the first of our children grew in her womb. I have a clear memory of the flawless skin, bright eyes and shining, thick hair as the pregnancy ripened.

Gareth Evan Palmer was born on 3rd June 1959, weighed in at 9lbs. 11ozs, both child and mother safe and healthy. It should be mentioned that Joan had fifteen stitches after the birth needed by such a large baby. The only plus factor, apart from the car to ferry my family around, was that Joan's failure to breast feed her son was easily remedied by the gift from my employers of 96 cans of Carnation milk which helped my son begin his physical growth towards the stature of sixteen stones that he attained in adulthood.

It was not long before the sinister Mr Treadle, Area Manager for Carnation and I had a showdown. Previous Sales Managers I had known had all had big happy personalities, smiling their way through my life in shop demonstrations and sales conferences, and maintaining their equanimity even when saying unpleasant things about my many failures to come up to the mark as a salesman. I remember Smith and Lowrie were both extremely likeable characters. Mr Treadle was a very different cup of tea. In the relatively short space of our acquaintance he never smiled once. His deadpan face gave nothing away, but he did a sort of sneering chuckle to accompany the snide remarks and sarcasm which eventually caused me to leave Carnation. The thing that precipitated the move was a suggestion that I had lied to him. The week before this incident he had appointed a rendezvous with me outside Thomas and Evans in High street, Bargoed at 0930hrs. I was and am always early at such times and although I was dreading the date, I was there with at least ten minutes to spare. At twenty to ten, I decided to proceed with the call. As usual, all my attempts to sell and leave a POS display were rejected in about five minutes, so I left the shop and waited a further five minutes in the car. Treadle did not show up. Just before 1000hrs I left and carried on with my other calls in Ystrad Mynach and Caerphilly. I finished the day's work and got home at around four in the afternoon. There was a phone message waiting for me from Treadle instructing me to report to him in the Angel Hotel at six that evening.

Joan, who had never met him, told me that he did not sound a very nice person and spent hardly

Chapter 3 / QUAKER OATS LTD

a minute on the phone, ending the call with, "Tell your husband, he had better not keep me waiting." She looked at me, obviously worried, but I smiled back at her reassuringly and changed the subject. I was early for my appointment at the hotel. On the way I fumed at Treadle's rudeness to Joan, half making up my mind to snatch the initiative and finish with Carnation straightaway. However, I decided to listen to him first. I found his Room number at reception and unannounced, went up to see him.

A single knock at his door brought immediate response as the door swung open he said, "Well, Palmer. Why were you not at Thomas and Evans? You had better come in." He turned and walked in front of me into the room.

"Where were you at ten to ten this morning, Mr Treadle? Not at High Street Bargoed, because I waited there for you before I made that call." He looked at me, surprised and alarmed, noticing the aggression in my voice. "Did you go into the outlet and check with Mr Hughes? If you had, he would have confirmed I had called" There was a pause as he realised I was not submitting to his nasty tone.

"Sit down, Carl. I know I was late this morning, but I thought you might have waited for me" He smiled his sickly insincere smile, and in my heart, I knew I had won round one. He was conciliatory because I had guessed right, he had not gone in to see the manager at Bargoed.

I took a seat at the table in his room and waited for him to proceed. He had been wrong-footed by my attack and I saw the effect of it by the confusion in the way he suggested that I was not doing very well as reflected by the empty pages in my order book. I was ready for this and complained that I had only been on the territory for three weeks.

From retailer responses, I had found out that I was not the first rep, to try to oppose Nestle in the valleys, and from the complete absence of any stocks of evaporated milks of other than Ideal milk, I knew that other sales teams had met the same stony resistance I had.

"Mr Treadle, you have not answered my question. Why did you not go in to check on me in Bargoed?" With great delight, I saw his face redden." I'll tell you why. Shall I ? You knew you would have had no more success than I would." I knew I had him.

"That isn't the point, Carl, but there is no point in crying over spilt milk. I was annoyed to have missed you this morning." he paused uncomfortably, but I hadn't finished with him yet.

"What upset me more than anything else, was the rude way you spoke to my wife when you phoned her. You knew she has not long had our baby and she was quite tearful when I got home. What did

Chapter 3 / QUAKER OATS LTD

you mean by saying, "He had better not keep me waiting?"

Once again I had surprised Treadle. Red-faced, he apologised and I could tell I had thrown him. There must have been other times when his bullying had been challenged: when there had been complaints to Head office.

Snatching my chance, I brought matters to a head by saying, "I will not put up with treatment like this, Mr Treadle, I resign."

He was not slow to see that this was a chance for his escape too.

"I am very sorry you have decided to take this course, Carl. I certainly did not mean to be rude to your wife. I hope you will convey my apologies to her." I made no reply to this.

"Well, I suppose I must with regret, accept your resignation. I will arrange for your salary to be paid to the end of the month, I hope you find this acceptable."

Within half an hour, I had handed over order books, advertising files and of course, my car to him and as I left his room, he said, "I am sorry things did not work out, Carl." He held out his hand to me and I shook it, pleased to be quitting selling once again. I knew this time that I had learned my lesson. When I got home, on the bus, of course, Joan was anxiously waiting and her first reaction when I told her I had resigned surprised me.

"Thank God for that."

THE ADJUTANT WINKED AT ME / *Carl Palmer*

This was followed by a worried face, and the question "What will you do, then, love?"

Although I laughed and quickly reassured her, in my heart I was worried. My CV was beginning to look like a Joke book, and I knew it would be difficult to get work quickly. My parents were on holiday at this time, which meant that I did not have to tell them anything about being out of work. I knew my father would be furious and accuse me of being irresponsible: I'd have to plead guilty to that. I remember sleeping hardly at all that night.

I applied for over sixty jobs in the fortnight ahead. Gardener/Handyman, Shop assistant in several shops, many clerks posts, Trainee driving instructor, and as a Factory operator. I left home early every morning to report to the Cardiff Labour Exchange, instantly available for work of any sort. I must have had at least twenty interviews and heard almost daily of failure "to satisfy" the panel. I began to panic, but the one certainty I had up my sleeve was the taxi driving job which I knew I could take up at a moments notice. The wage was only six pounds per week, but the tips would double, or even treble that.

One of my earliest applications had been for the post of TCA (Temporary Clerical Assistant) in the District Valuers Office, a Civil Service concern in

Chapter 3 / QUAKER OATS LTD

Llanishen, Cardiff. A very kindly older man had interviewed me, but though he seemed kindly enough, I had heard nothing. At the beginning of my third week of unemployment, when my morale was sinking fast, the post man brought good news with a OHMS letter. I was offered the TCA post for which I had applied, starting work straightaway.

Joan cried, so did I. I had been saved again.

It was another of those occasions when I was tearfully grateful to acknowledge the power of prayer.

4

BIRTH AND REBIRTHS

When my first child, Gareth, was a year old, my wife said to me, "Are you going to be a bum all your life; in a dull job with no prospects, just enjoying Amateur dramatics and allowing me to be the career person? It's not good enough, Carl?

I came to my senses. The date was December 1960 and for me, my Renaissance. With meagre qualifications from school; with a Gold medal in the speaking of verse and prose, with a rising reputation as a theatre director in the Am Dram movement in Cardiff, I made the obvious choice. One day, on my way home from my boring Temp Clerical Asst post in the civil service in Llanishen, a suburb of Cardiff, I arranged an interview with the Principal of Cardiff Training College, W.T.Jones. He was a lovely man and most understanding. He listened to my tale of woe and said, "If you study for the June A level exam in English and get a Pass grade, I will admit you as a mature student on a Teacher Training course in September."

In January 1961, I enrolled, 18 months late for the "A" level course at Llandaff Tech and took to it like a duck to water. Motivation was the spur! I worked with complete concentration and huge enjoyment. From my prozaic existence, I had found a chance to lift myself into the teaching profession. What a chance, perhaps the last chance!

Joan was pregnant again, with our second child in those early months of 1961. She always looked radiantly fit when pregnant. We were both excited at the possibility that her dormant lazy lump of a husband might at last emerge with a promising career. She had been the instigator and I was determined not to fail her. Shakespeare, Chaucer, D.H.Lawrence and Arthur Miller were the set works and I devoured them. The bit was between my teeth now and nightly trips to the pub were filled with literary appreciation and testing each other on the texts. This was possible because a young chorister friend was also studying "A" level.

As Joan's pregnancy ripened, so did my rebirth as a student of English. The three papers at A level were taken in June '61 and in late August, my huge-bellied wife rushed down stairs on hearing the let-

Chapter 4 / BIRTH AND REBIRTHS

ters drop. She turned, beamed brightly up at me and yelled "You have passed, love"

Our joy was complete when I rang the Training College with news of my success. A place had been reserved for me to read English and Drama for the Certificate of Education. All being well I could become a teacher. My dilettante years ended, I prepared not only for our second child, but by eagerly swotting at the recommended reading for my new course. I continued my Civil Service job for as long as I could, that is until the second week in September when I was due to start college.

My grant application had been sent as soon as my exam results had arrived and at the end of August, I was pleased to learn that my first year grant would be £620 pa. This was a great relief because we had a mortgage payment of £10 per month on our little terraced house in an old part of Cardiff. I had taken a part time job as a taxi driver in Glamtax and I knew they would be glad to use me on the weekends in term time. This would be a most welcome extra income. All looked promising in my life, as I nervously approached Cardiff Training College on September 14, 1961.

I felt embarrassed at my balding head and advanced years (I was 27) as I saw a crowd of young people talking loudly and for the most part in broad Welsh accents. I had a mac over my arm, a shirt and tie and sports coat and grey flannels on. From my early years, I have always worn a hat, and as I looked at the black blazers with newly sewn badges and bulging physiques, I felt completely out of place. Some of the young women were Cardiffian, and I soon got into conversation with them, but they were so much younger than me that it did not help much. Seven years difference at that age is a huge gap. Brian Dixon, from Porth and I got chatting, and as he was reading English like me, we soon became friends. A gaggle of young Cardiff girls turned up, some of them very attractive and the prospect of getting to know them as fellow students made the day suddenly seem more exciting. We were shortly processed and gathered together in the dilapidated hall of the canteen-dining room.

Two young friends I soon made, were to become famous. The tall, dark and handsome man from Maesteg was, like me going to read English as well as PE. His name was Lyn Davies who earned world fame as an Olympic champion and Roy Noble, another English student, would become a much-loved broadcaster on BBC Wales. On that morning, however, we were all nervous and awkward with each other as we jostled for position. My gratitude at being a day student was shared by the crowd into

Chapter 4 / BIRTH AND REBIRTHS

which Brian Dixon and I had established ourselves, because we, at least could go home tonight.

Joan was due to produce my first daughter at any time, and she had opted to have the baby at home. I was anxious to waste no time with these kids as I thought of them, and get home to her. My son, Gareth was just over two and I wanted to be home to help Joan with him. With a handful of forms to fill in, one of which had upset me because it had made clear that all students, unless they could provide medical evidence, would be expected to participate in a PE session once a week. I escaped from the college in Heath Park and walked the mile home. I had never been keen on PE and I made up my mind to go to my doctor with my old knee complaint and ask him for a certificate which would exempt me from PE.

The induction as a student had been far less painful than I had expected and as I have often found, I had no trouble in finding friends in college. The other statistic that worried me about that first day was that I found I was the only man doing Main Drama, with thirteen girls to keep me company, all of them about eighteen years old. The gap between 18 and 27 is a chasm at that age, but nine years later in life, is no distance at all. As I remember how beautiful some of those girls were, I am very grateful I did not know then what I know now, otherwise the course of my personal history would certainly have changed.

The timetable was made up of English and Drama lectures and practical sessions, Health education, Educational Psychology and PE. I soon adapted to the regime after my A level study, I had discovered a new enthusiasm for reading, so that my early written submissions earned above average grades. I was relieved and encouraged by this. The staff were friendly and I noticed that my advanced age and married status gained me a friendly attitude from the staff. We were told our first teaching practice would take place after Christmas, in the spring of 62. We were required to chose our own level in schools placements; either Infant Junior, or Secondary Junior, so I opted for the latter.

The lectures, of one hour duration were almost all enjoyable and stimulating. This was confirmation to me that my decision to enter teaching had been the right one. Education as a subject of study was divided into sections loosely, History and Practice. I soon realised that the Practice was what I preferred. But we were constantly reminded that there would be no award of teaching certificate without passes in Theory. There was a gentle and kindly man called Roberts, who was the Principal Education Lecturer and it was the fear of losing his

Chapter 4 / BIRTH AND REBIRTHS

support that made me strive manfully to excel in both Theory and Practice of Education.

Here I must pause to describe the arrival of my first daughter, Dyfi, (pronounced DUVEE) into the world. Our boy had been born in a Maternity Hospital in 1959, but this new baby was to be born at home, a small terraced house in the suburbs. A team of nurse and midwife had been engaged, but our GP had persuaded Joan to have the baby under hypnosis, so she had been attending sessions with him and was quite happy about the prospect.

At about 2300hrs on the 18th September, a Sunday night, Joan's labour pains started and, unruffled, she told me to phone the doctor. Within 15 minutes, the doctor arrived and went up to our bedroom, where he spent twenty minutes with Joan, as I waited listening downstairs in the hall. When he came down he said to me, "It's alright Carl. I've put her under for a while and told her when she wakes, you would have the power to put her to sleep again. OK?"

I gulped and said," Yes doctor, but how do I do it?" He smiled," Don't worry. Just sit on the side of the bed, hold one of her hands and with the other hand, you stroke her forehead and say 'One two three four five. One two three four five, One two three four five', 'til she goes off to sleep again, Got it?' I smiled thinly." If you say so, doctor."

"You've got the nurses' number, haven't you?"
"Yes, "I said.

A second's pause and he was gone.

It was a chilly autumn night as I closed the front door, but I was covered in sweat. I sat down in my silent living room, hardly daring to breathe. I was beginning to relax half an hour later, "Carl, Carl" It was not yet midnight, as I hurried upstairs" Alright, love I'm coming." She was sitting on the side of the bed holding her side. I moved quickly round the bed to sit beside her. "Lie down again, love"

"She looked at me, unbelieving.

I lifted her legs and gently swung them and her body, until she was lying on the bed again

"What are you doing? I've started labour pains again."

I smoothed her forehead with my right hand and began, "One two three four five, One two three …."

She turned her head roughly away and said, in the furious voice I knew so well. "Don't be silly, Carl".

"Ring the nurses, now." I rose from the bed.

"Go on, love. I'll be alright."

Defeated, but fully alert, I ran downstairs. I rang the Maternity number. The clock in the living room stood at 12.20.

Chapter 4 / BIRTH AND REBIRTHS

For the longest half hour of my life, I waited upstairs with Joan. I had never felt more impotent. When our doorbell rang at ten to one, I was there before the echo died.

Two rather short, blue-hatted and blue-uniformed girls stood in the porch.

"I'm Muriel and her name is Olwen," said the one in front pushing past me into the hall.

"I'm Carl. My wife's upstairs. I have to tell you she's having the baby under hypnosis," I said.

"Oh, that's nice. You go and put the kettle on. We'll be down in a minute." I heard subdued laughs, and they both vanished upstairs.

I have a clear memory of a huge sense of relief, as I heard Muriel say to my wife. "Hello, love. Let's have a look at you then."

I stepped lively into the kitchen and put the kettle on. I did not make the tea until I heard them clumping downstairs in their nurses sensible shoes ten minutes later.

"I've given her a shot of pethidine, and she's gone back to sleep. What did you say your name was? How about some toast then, lovey? We might have a long wait."

Muriel smiled at me and sank into my armchair as Olwen sat at the dining table. I felt happy that the situation was now out of my hands.

"I'm Carl, dear. Tea and toast is on the way. Thanks for coming so quickly."

THE ADJUTANT WINKED AT ME / Carl Palmer

We chatted about my early days in college. Time passed pleasantly enough. They both had plenty of stories about their working parishes around Cardiff. Two further pots of tea, about thirty cigarettes, a bottle of red wine I had been saving for the occasion and a sudden lull brought the bombshell question, "You have remembered about the placenta, haven't you?" said Muriel.

No, I had not remembered. What was I to do? I had been told that after the birth, the nursing team would give the father a parcel containing the placenta or some would say, the afterbirth, because it was his job to dispose of it. This was, almost always by placing it on the coal fire burning in the grate. For weeks now, I had known this and had been meaning to order my coal, so that I would be able to burn it as prescribed. I had not ordered the coal, and I began to panic as to what I would do.

"Yes, don't worry" I said. I even managed a smile.

As the girls continued chatting, I scrabbled in my mind. Yes. The shed at the bottom of the garden, already dilapidated, had to be sacrificed.

"Sh, sh," said Muriel. "It's Joan. Come on, Olwen." They dashed out of the room.

It was just after 0430hrs, and I began to wonder if I could manage to give the shed the death blow with the few tools I had.

Chapter 4 / BIRTH AND REBIRTHS

For a half hour I scraped nearly half a bucket of coal dust from the floor of the coal house. I screwed newspaper and magazine paper into tightly compressed pellets and pushed them into the bottom of the grate. It was still silent upstairs. My watch showed 0500hrs when I stepped across our tatty garden to deal with the shed. I managed to unscrew the hinges on the shed door and lie it on the floor of the garden without making much noise, but now I had not to think of my sleeping neighbours any longer. Picking up the coal-breaking axe, I dealt the side of the shed a fearsome blow, then another and another; it yielded. Frantically, I started to hammer the planks of which it was made into pieces of kindling. At that moment I was aware of bedroom lights flickering on to my left and right. Sensibly seeing a demented man with an axe in his hand, no one interfered. It was hard work for about an hour as the eight foot planks of wood were transformed into pieces small enough to serve their unusual purpose. I carried them into the living room aware that my work must have disturbed what was going on in our bedroom; my secret was out too, for the nurses would have realised why the noise in the garden had been necessary. As I laid the fire in the grate, I uttered a prayer of thanks in advance for my new child.

Just before six, I had readied the fire, but I waited until Olwen's face appeared at the kitchen door to say the baby was about to arrive. She then left to help with the birth. I heard my new daughter's cry at 6.55 am, and that was just after I had lit the fire, which was now blazing away. Muriel shouted for me to come and see them and I rushed up to see Olwen holding my little girl whose face was still screwed up so tightly, apprehensive in this new world. Joan was white-faced with effort and tiredness.

"Are you all right, love?" I said. She smiled thinly and nodded.

"What's her name?" Muriel asked.

"Dyfi," said Joan. "We never thought of any other name. We both love it."

"I can't stay love. I've got the fire lit." I leaned over the bed and kissed her. I love you, Joan Palmer."

"She was 9lb 11oz" Muriel said to my back, as I left the bedroom, and started to cry at the thought of my wife's bravery.

Gareth had been a big baby, too, I remembered as I hurried back to the fire. Within half an hour, Muriel came down with a parcel the size of a large family pack of fish and chips wrapped in newspaper. "Over to you, Dad," she said. Gingerly, I accepted the heavy pack and immediately placed it on the blazing fire, which, frequently stoked with small shovelfuls of coal, and new lengths of dry timber soon did the job it had been prepared for.

Chapter 4 / BIRTH AND REBIRTHS

Gareth had slept through the night of his sister's birth, and woke by eight, by which time the nurses and I had had toast and tea, the documentation had been completed, and Muriel had phoned her HQ and the social services department, who would provide our home help, a Mrs. Steward, who would help us cope with our first week as a family of four.

As Muriel and Olwen joked with me, I changed Gareth's nappy, washed him and gave him his breakfast. I felt completely happy that this special night had been successfully accomplished. The girls were given two bottles of wine I had bought for the occasion and telling me to let Joan sleep for as long as I could, both of them kissed me and walked out of our life.

The first phone call was to, my parents, who told me that they would spread the news. The second was to Dr Jones, whose receptionist agreed to ask to visit us later, perhaps before lunch. I sat down and watched Gareth playing with his wooden bricks, as I rang the college to tell them that I would not be in till later in the week. I then realised how exhausted I was, had another cup of tea and buttered toast and marmalade. Hearing sounds from our bedroom, I carried Gareth upstairs to see his new sister. We peeped round the bedroom door to see that Joan with her hand on the rim of the Moses basket was already asleep again. I tip-toed across the room with Gareth and together we looked in at Dyfi who was also asleep. "There's your sister son. Do you like her?"

"Wossa name?" he whispered.

"Dyfi" I said.

He laughed. "That's a funny name, Dyfi."

Those first weeks of my daughter's life were made easy by the presence of our help, Mrs. Steward, who arrived at 0845hrs on the morning that Dyfi was born. She cleaned, washed, cooked for us as though we were her own. She came from North Wales, had a daughter of her own, and was in her early fifties. We soon respected and loved her, for, without any supervision, she ran the domestic side of our life as Joan became stronger and recovered. She had needed thirteen stitches, so it was a painful time for her. Mrs. Steward insisted on her resting and fiercely guarded her convalescent time like her real mother. Within minutes of starting work, she asked in that easy North Wales accent. "Goot 'eavens, what on earth haf you got a fire for?" When I explained about my early morning shed demolition to burn the after-birth, she giggled for days.

The other huge advantage of having help at home, was that I was able to return to college by Wednesday lunchtime though Joan did not want me to go back so early. It was a short afternoon of

Chapter 4 / BIRTH AND REBIRTHS

lectures and I was feeling conscience-stricken, so I went, but was soon back home again.

My pleasure in becoming used to the academic life after years of mind-numbing boredom was acute. As I have already said I found no difficulty in the Drama lectures, because of my experience in broadcasting and producing plays, so that many of the "kitchen sink" plays were already known to me, as were the works of Arthur Miller, Tennessee Williams, Priestly , Shaw and Shakespeare. Our Drama lecturer was a gentle man, not much older than me and we soon became mutually respectful. "Gay" was a word which meant "jolly" in those days, and I'm afraid his sexuality seemed to favour the Oscar Wilde school, but that did not detract from his professional ability. It was my obvious familiarity with Theatre and stage technical terms, that impressed him, as did my acting ability and my speech which betrayed the fact that "I had done a bit".

My first colossal mistake in my college life resulted from my stage knowledge and big mouth! One afternoon, the Drama lecturer was away, so a Senior lecturer from the English department stood in for his lecture with us. I was the only other man present, so there were nine girls for him to impress. In his late forties, this man decided to impress with his wide range of knowledge. I cringed as he made wildly inaccurate attempts to describe stage and lighting terms. "Does anyone know what the proper term is for the lights above us?" he leered at us, proud of his superior know how. I did not attempt to tell him. I smelled danger. He pointed to the spots in the auditorium at right and left. "Those are called house lights, and the lights you see above us are the stage lights."

By this time, I was finding it hard to restrain myself. The last information he had given us was rubbish --- completely untrue, and if he gave us any more evidence of his ignorance about stage terms, I was going to feel compelled to correct him. It was not a question of my showing off about my theatre knowledge, it was because I was outraged that this opinionated twerp thought he could get away with waffling about a subject, the only subject I was qualified in, and therefore close to my heart. The lights above our heads were floodlights, the lights to left and right in the auditorium were called FOH, or Front of House lights.

He strode to the wings at stage right, and turned the winder, closing the curtains. He was obviously enjoying himself.
"Does anyone know what these are called?" he asked, dramatically holding on to the curtains to which he was referring. A courageous girl in front of me, decide to chance her luck.

Chapter 4 / BIRTH AND REBIRTHS

"Curtains?" she said.

He smiled at her indulgently, "Yes, we can all see that, my dear. But what are they called in theatre terms?" he was a silly voice again, and I wanted to wipe the smile off his face.

He said, "They are called Flats."

"Tabs," I said, loud enough for everyone to hear.

All heads turned towards me. His eyes bored into mine as the silence stretched, as the blush grew on his face and I knew I had made an enemy for life.

"Mr. Palmer isn't it?" he asked. "Well done, just testing. They are called "Tabs".

"Now I think you had all better note these technical terms I have given you. When you have done that, we will begin the play reading."

I knew I had made a serious mistake in correcting him. For the next three years in college he made my life as uncomfortable as he could. More to the point, he never again stood in for the Drama lecturer. He knew I had found him out and he would never forgive me for it. There was no avoiding him, for I was a student in his department in which he specialised in poetry. His spite was to dog my steps, and I became paranoid in his lectures, even when I longed to answer a question he put to us, fear and prudence prevented me from volunteering anything at all. Aside from this, I found the lectures stimulating and the teaching practices were a thrill

THE ADJUTANT WINKED AT ME / Carl Palmer

as I found I could enthuse the pupils and, consequently, "job well done" glows at the end of the practice days.

Of course, my sharpest pleasure came from Drama lessons during those "pracs", when the skills I had learned in acting, stage-craft, and the interpretations of playwrights' works in big groups in Cardiff and Swansea gave me advantage, over younger students. The only silly part of the situation in Drama sessions in college, was that I was the only man. In improvisation it was a heavy credulity-stretch that the male part was always played by me. The fact that I was nine years older than all the girls in the group made some of the situations ludicrous. Our lecturer had a knack for inventing the oddest scenarios for some of our improvisations and often made me think he deliberately had me in mind when he invented them!

I remember being really shy as I played a spider underneath a table around which eight girls were sitting. I can remember gazing at close quarters, at eight pairs of delicious girls' knees and deciding which ones to tickle with the feather I had been given. It was, needless to say a chance, any other male student in college would have given his eye teeth for. As it was, I tickled a few ankles and calves, and the inside of the knee of the girl from whom I knew would come a huge shriek, and quickly

Chapter 4 / BIRTH AND REBIRTHS

emerged, red faced and rudely grinning. There were also public performances in the college hall, from time to time, but, as I have already explained, I shunned attempts to recruit me for anything but the smallest of parts.

My family life was really happy as the new baby Dyfi, took her place in it. We were four now, and the work I did as a taxi driver at the weekends, helped to maintain a good standard of living. There was no time for the making of friendships among my fellow students, and in any case, their social lives were spent with people of their own age who were also living in.

For someone who spent years searching for something he could enjoy doing for a living to discover such enjoyment in teaching was a hugely significant development. My age and experience of the world of work, gave me an authority amongst children, and I found no difficulty in gaining and holding pupils' attention, so the prospect of doing this full time was exciting. Both types of school interested me, but my understandable preference was to apply for secondary level where my life experience in Drama would serve me, and my pupils best.

In those early sixties, corporal punishment was frequently used, and though I did not relish using it myself, I observed how effective it was amongst rude and rebellious children. It was comforting to know that a really effective deterrent to bad behaviour existed.

By the time I had adjusted to college life, I was well into my second year, having done reasonably well in the first year papers, though my marks in English confirmed that I was never going to be able to expect high marks. In the theory papers in Education, I had done well. The lecturers were kind, because my ability in teaching prac had been acknowledged. In English, my comprehension and vocabulary work was well rewarded, but in literature, my marks were barely satisfactory, of course, in poetry criticism, my implacable enemy was pleased to be able to find my attempts to appraise poems slight and shallow. (How I came to hate that man!)

Around Spring '64, Joan told me we were expecting again. By this time, the final teaching practice was in sight, and final exams meant swotting to prepare for the June papers. My anticipation of finding a teaching post for the September of that year, i.e., 1964, filled my mind, as I journeyed to a secondary school in Llandaff where I was to spend my final teaching prac, of six weeks duration. I had made a preliminary visit two weeks previously, when the Deputy Head, a lady English teacher, had told me I would be working with her for English and Drama

Chapter 4 / BIRTH AND REBIRTHS

lessons. She was a stern formidable woman, well past middle age, a stickler for discipline and unmarried (I knew because she told me so). I observed her technique during a double period on that first day and could see that the fourth form really liked her and responded in oral work impressively. Out of the blue, Miss Hore (Bless her, for that was the cross she had to bear), asked me to read Wordsworth's Westminster Bridge to the class. She must have guessed it would be a gift for me. When I had finished reading, there was a strange silence. I looked at her alarmed as she said, "Form Four, that is the way a poem should be read, don't you think Mr. Palmer deserves a clap for showing us how to do it?" Of course, I was delighted by the loud applause and the smiling pupils, and deeply impressed by Miss Hore's generous spirit.

From that moment, my work with all age groups in the school was daily vindication of my decision to become a teacher. The staff were also warm in their welcome. It was not unusual for students on teaching prac. to tell stories of not being allowed to use staffrooms, and of having to wait in draughty corridors for morning and afternoon breaks. In my school, Miss Hore took me into the staffroom on that first morning and made it clear that I was welcome to use it whenever I was free.

THE ADJUTANT WINKED AT ME / Carl Palmer

In keeping with the procedure of being observed by Education Department lecturers, I was subjected to regular visits and, with growing excitement, I became aware that they all approved my work. The big bonus came as my stay in the school was beginning to wane, I was told to prepare for a team of external examiners to visit during my last double period at the school. All of us knew that team visits usually meant that a Distinction grade was highly likely. I was thrilled. When I told Miss Hore, she said, "I am not at all surprised. Well done!"

For the visit, I had prepared a huge staged improvisation by the Fourth Form. Everything went well and as I turned towards the audience on the final curtain I was dismayed to find three people I had never met and the one lecturer whom I did not wish to meet. I think he spotted the uneasy look on my face because he smiled at me and gave me the thumbs up sign. Could I have been wrong about him for the past three years? I didn't think so. Of course, the visitors left without a word to me; just a smile and a nod.

I was really embarrassed to be presented with a card and a sweet pewter tankard by the Fourth Form. A beautiful, blue-eyed girl said to me after kissing me a shade too enthusiastically," You'll be a great teacher, Mr. Palmer!" Of course, I cried. It was Miss Hore who put the icing on my cake.

Chapter 4 / BIRTH AND REBIRTHS

After telling me not to hesitate to use her name as a referee, she said, "I had a word with the chief examiner before they left. He told me there were only four Distinctions for teaching prac in your year group, so I asked him the obvious question. Yes Mr. Palmer, you are one of them." As I walked home to Joan that evening, I was truly proud of the fact that, at last, I had found my place in the working world.

The final exams came and went. The brightest candidates could expect to be offered an extra year to qualify as Bachelors of Education. There was never any doubt in my mind that my work was not more than satisfactory. No clues were given as to marks attained in the few lectures in English. Excellent pupils were singled out for mention, but my implacable enemy on the staff did not even look in my direction. The suspense was agonizing. I will not be persuaded that some lecturers know very well the worry that their delays cause and seize on these opportunities to distress as their sadistic right!

I had spotted a vacancy in the local sec. mod. Ty Celyn, advertised in the newspaper, so had sent off for an application form and quickly submitted it. I made an appointment with one of the Education lecturers whom I knew from my grammar school days. When we met, I was surprised to find that he remembered my name, not only that, but he had heard of my teaching prac. prowess.

"You know who is the Head of Ty Celyn, do you, Carl? Its Arthur Hill."

"He taught me History, Sir." I replied.

"I'll give him a ring tonight. Tell him about your final prac. That should give you a good start, Carl."

"I haven't had my English results yet, Sir, so don't promise him too much,"

"I don't think you'll have much to worry about there. You've sent in your application form, have you?"

"Yes, Sir."

"Don't worry about the English results. They always sit on their papers longer than any of the rest of us." said this kindly man, without any idea of how his comments had encouraged me.

Within the week I had been invited to interview for the job, at the Education offices in Cardiff City Hall. On the Friday afternoon before the Monday of my interview, my Education friend sent for me to come and see him.

"Something to cheer you up, Carl. I had a word with Hywel (Head of Education dept.) who told me you're recommended for a distinction. All you need now is a pass in English." He smiled.

Chapter 4 / BIRTH AND REBIRTHS

"Thank you Mr. B I'm very grateful to you. We're expecting our third in September, so it's important for me to get work"

"Don't worry about the English result. Hywel told me "the school that gets you will be a lucky one."

I left his office feeling very pleased with myself, though still worried about English. When I got to the City Hall on the morning of the interview, there were two other candidates waiting, a man in his early forties and a young woman. Before we had time for a chat, a clerk appeared and asked the man in for his interview. The girl and I talked. She was already in post as a Drama teacher in a Welsh medium school in Cardiff. She said she was nervous, as the subjects she could offer were Drama and R.I., and the advert had asked for English and Drama. I made no comment, but my heart lifted because I offered the specified subjects.

After about a quarter of an hour, the man emerged with a grim expression for both of us. The clerk, holding the door open summoned the girl in. My companion said, "Pretty short interview. There are only two of them and the clerk. The Head asked most of the questions. I'm an English teacher, and all they asked about was about my experience of teaching Drama. In a cross voice, he added. "I dunno why they asked me for interview."

"Where d'you teach?" I asked.

"I'm number two in the English dept at Rhydfelen. Where are you teaching?"

"I've just finished in the Training college." I said.

He smiled and gave a sort of grunt, which I interpreted as satisfaction at the feebleness of the opposition..

The office door opened to the sight of the girl turned towards the panel to say, "Thank you very much," she walked to us smiling confidently.

"Mr Palmer, please, "said the clerk and I followed him into the room.

"Behind a very large desk, sat the familiar face of one of Cardiff's senior aldermen. At his left, sat the large and well-remembered Arthur Hill, who had unsuccessfully taught me History. The clerk sat at the Chairman's right, burying his head in his papers.

"Yes, I do remember you" said the Head. "This is the Chairman, Alderman Hedley-Poulter." Hedley-Poulter raised heavy-lidded eyes towards me, grunted and continued his examination of my application form, which I knew to be far from impressive.

"Bit late to change direction, isn't it?" He did not trouble to hide the scorn in his voice. He was MD of a big Cardiff company, and I thought, "how could a fat smelly dinosaur like him be deemed capable of judging the relative merits of teachers?"

Chapter 4 / BIRTH AND REBIRTHS

"Yes Sir. But I found my college course has shown I have something to offer as a teacher."

This of course, was a prepared answer. He made no reply. Silence. He looked up at me for a few seconds, grunted and said, "Arthur"

Mr Hill smiled at me, almost apologetically and said, "Well Mr Palmer, Tell us about your experience in Drama.

With such a gift of a question, I was delighted and talked of my experience of acting and producing plays on the Forces Broadcasting service in Germany, and my few TV bit parts, then launched into my experience of acting in and producing plays in the professional theatres in Cardiff. It was at this point, that our venerable Alderman, rudely interrupted.

"Yes yes, yes alright. But what about teaching experience?"

"Well, of course," I began.

"I have spoken to the Education Department in college, about the candidate's potential, Sir" said the Head." They have assured me that his practical work is of outstanding quality."

There was a pause during which Hedley-Poulter snorted.

"Perhaps you can tell us how you enjoyed your teaching of English." said the Head.

At this point I explained that Miss Hore had helped me to shadow her teaching methods in

THE ADJUTANT WINKED AT ME / Carl Palmer

English with her own fourth form, I was thrilled to find how effective they were over the six weeks I had spent with her.

"Thank you, Carl." said the Head, rising to his feet. I think we know all we need to know now. Thank you for coming. Will you wait outside, please."

I said "Thank you, Sir". The clerk was already holding the door open for me.

"When I rejoined the other candidates, I was uncomfortably aware that my interview had taken no longer than either of theirs.

"How did it go?" asked the man from Rhydyfelen.

"Oh alright, I suppose. I didn't like the chairman of the panel. He contributed nothing." I replied.

"Yeah, typical old councillor, just a makeweight." he said.

I turned to smile at the girl. She smiled back, but said nothing. The three of us sat there deep in our own thoughts and waited.

I had plenty to think about. Joan was expecting me home for lunch and I knew how disappointed she would be. She worked so hard in keeping our kids clean and doing all the housework herself. Now she was manifestly pregnant again, and I felt really guilty that I was the one having an easy time as a student, while she ran the family single-handedly.

Chapter 4 / BIRTH AND REBIRTHS

It was so important for me to take the good news home to Joan, and as the minutes ticked by I began to be sure I was not going to be the successful candidate. Had I done enough in preparation for the interview? Should I have tried to canvas - at least my own ward councillor? My mind was in a torment as I waited. There had been no other vacancies in Cardiff schools and I began to believe the only thing to do would be to move. We didn't want to do that. We had very little money saved, and we were comfortably able to afford the mortgage we had. Perhaps the most important reason of all was that we enjoyed living in Cardiff.

I looked at my watch and was shocked to find my interview had ended fifteen minutes ago. What could be holding them up? Could there be an extra candidate for whom they were waiting? I looked at the other male interviewee and raised my eyebrows in question. He replied with a similar wordless gesture. The door to the interview room opened, to reveal the ancient, bloated figure of Hedley-Poulter.

"I'll see you here next week for the Deputy Heads panel, Arthur," he boomed far too loudly. Virtually slamming the door behind him, and without a glance at the bench on which we sat, exuding an air of whisky and stale tobacco, he strode slowly down the corridor and out of our lives.

THE ADJUTANT WINKED AT ME / *Carl Palmer*

With a covert glance at each other, we tensed, expecting a summons for one of us at any moment. The door opened and the clerk came out, appeared to have forgotten something and went back in, but left the door open." You want the other two to wait," we heard plainly. He reappeared, looked down at his list, turned to us and said, "Will you come in, Mr. Palmer? Perhaps you two would stay there for the moment; we won't keep you long" My heart nearly bursting with joy, but as yet, apprehensive, I followed the clerk into the room.

"Sorry to have kept you waiting young Palmer," Arthur Hill said, standing up from his chair, extending his hand to me and smiling. "The post is yours if you want it. This is a firm offer of a permanent appointment with this authority. Do you accept it? I hope so, you had a very good interview." he took my hand. "Thank you very much, Sir, of course I accept," I said. His handshake was firm as he smiled at me and said, "I am sure you will be very happy with us, Carl. I know you will fit in very well."

Walking to the bus stop, I had time to feel sorry for the other two candidates, but was mainly concerned with proving to the Head that he had made a wise choice. Joan was speechless with joy when I told her. We just sat there looking at each other, hugging each other with sheer pleasure that things had turned out so well.

Chapter 4 / BIRTH AND REBIRTHS

After we had lunched, I rang the education dept to thank Mr. B and ask whether the English results were yet published - they were not. At noon on the last day of college, just before we were due to go to the local pub for a farewell drink, the long-awaited results were displayed on the notice board. No one had failed, to my intense relief I had obtained a 'C' grade which was all I needed. My prayers had been answered. God is good.

It was nearly three weeks after I started teaching that our last baby was born. It had been a lovely summer; lovely because of the excitement in the air. We were waiting for the baby and, for the first time, I was excited about starting work. Only three months earlier we had moved house. The new home was still only a terraced house, but had cost twice the price of our first house. We paid the colossal sum of £3,600 for it as it was of more modern construction and was in a "gardens" i.e., it had a wide grassed area in front of it. The mortgage payments had gone up to £17 2s 11d per month, but on my teacher's salary, I could just afford it.

Joan had had a trouble-free pregnancy and we were both thrilled at the thought of a new baby. Joan had become a most loving mother and, now that she could feel confident about our financial future, she faced the prospect of our becoming a five-some with great pleasure. Nappies, Moses basket, cot and baby linen were now part of our inventory as we waited for our new arrival. We were now thirty years old and I soon became acclimatised to my role as a teacher, and not-so-young expectant dad. The baby was expected at the end of September and, though we were used to late births, we both felt that this one would be on time.

The weather was still warm, and both Gareth and Dyfi were looking forward to the new family member's arrival in the weekend before the due date. I had told my Head that I would phone him as soon as the action started, and probably be off for a few days. He readily agreed to this and my new colleagues were happy and accommodating.

It was on Tuesday September 27th that Joan, late in the evening, started to have labour pains. The children were in bed and asleep, and I was about to go to bed. These turned out to be a false alarm, so we went off to bed and pretended to go to sleep. At two thirty Joan shook my shoulder and told me to ring the midwife.

The team of two young nurses arrived at about half past three. Although I was beginning to panic, as soon as they were in my house, I relaxed. Unlike the drama of Dyfi's birth, everything went smoothly. Modern technology now dealt with the

Chapter 4 / BIRTH AND REBIRTHS

disposal of the placenta, and, quietly, at the respectable hour of 0740, Catrin Palmer joined the family. I remember noticing that special new birth smell had an extra fragrance to it as I was invited to see mother and child. My new daughter did not have that bright red colour that seems to be common to babies. She had a black, soft quiff of hair and looked as though she was still part of her mother. As the sun came into the bedroom lighting the scene, I felt supremely happy to welcome this lovely little milky creature into our lives. At 8 lbs 4oz, she was lighter than our other children, and Joan was able to breast feed her.

When I brought Dyfi and Gareth in to sit on the side of the bed, later, I felt not only a great sense of pride in my family, but a huge glow of gratitude in the providence that had, at last enabled me to get my career compass on course.

5

THE NORFOLK BROADS

The story you are about to read is not really funny, yet whenever I have related it to people, long before the end, they have all failed to prevent laughing out loud. It is a lot like the short stories of James Thurber, in that the things that happen over a short period of time, strain the credulity to breaking point. The rapid succession of disasters will hold the reader's interest, unable to believe that anything worse can happen; but, it can!

The rules have probably changed by now, but looking back, I am amazed that The Norfolk Broads Authority was prepared to risk peoples' safety as well as the expensive cruisers they offered for hire, on a brief and most inadequate period of instruction before licensing "Captains" and crews to cruise the Broads. If one of the consequences of writing this story is to deter future "sailors" from accepting the insanely skimpy, "what to do and how to do it", that I was given by an ill-qualified, careless, almost inarticulate oaf, then it has been worth my writing and you reading this. BON VOYAGE

I had always fancied myself in a white 'fore and aft' rig cap, glimpsed at the wheel of an expensive and powerful yacht coming alongside quaysides and 'tying up' before strolling side by side with my wife towards a riverside pub on The Broads.

The kids had grown up and left home and money were much easier. Joan had always resisted the idea, being very much a chic, small and attractive city woman who, like me, wouldn't know a reef knot from a Windsor knot, and had reached the age when nipping on and off a large and brand new river launch was, to say the least, a daunting and strenuous proposal. However, I prevailed, and accordingly booked a 'Santa Elena' class luxury, four berth power boat to be picked up at Reedham on the Broads for a week's hire. I sent off a cheque for £265 in the summer of 1981. We were in our late forties at the time, and from the moment I had booked the holiday, I was nervous.

Chapter 5 / THE NORFOLK BROADS

My friends on the staff at school were amused The Deputy Head of the School, my friend Bryan smilingly had a chat with me and taught me the need to learn knots, as it is essential to be able to tie a clove hitch on both mooring ropes (lines!) when pulling up to mooring places – clearly recognized by the posts (capstan) along the banks of the rivers. The R Yare was to be our main river going from Reedham winding towards Breyden water and thence through the middle of Great Yarmouth. "Remember," he said to me, "The rivers of the Broads are tidal, so, when you moor for the night, you must remember that."

As the end of term approached in the summer of '81, much joshing took place, and although my sense of humour has always been solid I could have done without it, because it undermined what little confidence I had in myself.

We were due to pick up the boat on Saturday lunchtime and take it back seven days later, so we left Cardiff at about 6am to complete the 250 miles journey in time for our rendezvous with the boat supervisor in Reedham. It was a long drive that Saturday morning. Conversation was rather limited as we drove eastwards from Cardiff and I knew my wife Joan was as nervous as I was, but being a more courageous person was determined not to show it, as we headed towards our first (and last) nautical adventure.

THE ADJUTANT WINKED AT ME / *Carl Palmer*

The boat yard was packed with cars when we arrived, and after finding an empty space, we parked our SAAB and walked towards a sign on the side of a smart looking building which read, "office". A young woman behind a desk greeted us with a good morning, asked our names, and ticking them off a sheet on a clip-board in front of her said "Mr. Hampson, won't be long. He's just on a demo run".

We sat, and within five minutes, the Mr. Hampson appeared and in that strange impenetrable Norwich accent said, "Royt, Mr. and Mrs. Paalmer, is it? Come with me folks." He smiled and with a hand gesture ushered us out of the door before him saying "She's all ready for you, valeted and fuelled up ready to go."

We walked beside him to where in a fifty or sixty yard basin, beautiful white motor launches were tied up by the stern to the bank. Our boat was no more than thirty yards from the office. I recognized it immediately from the brochure picture I had remembered, but it seemed much bigger than I had thought. It was just under thirty foot long and as we came to a halt at its mooring point I could not suppress a thrill of excitement at the adventure ahead.

Chapter 5 / THE NORFOLK BROADS

There was a five rung ladder hooked over a rail at the stern and, I gestured that Joan should go first. "No love," she said, with a quiet but urgent refusal. "You go first", so I did, then jumping down into the beautiful light brown strip-wood deck in the stern well, and nothing but the bench seating round its three sides, I turned and held up my hand to Joan, who had climbed the little ladder and now jumped down to join me.

Hampson did not attempt to join us so this was my first jerk of uneasiness as I looked down at him standing below us on the bank.

"Jeremy'll explain it all to you," Mr Hampson said. He reached up and handed me the clipboard. "When he's shown you the ropes and taken you for a handling run, he'll hand over to you, you can sign for her and be on your way. He won't be long." He turned on his heel and walked away. I turned to Joan who was sitting on the bench on the port (left hand) side of the boat, holding onto the rail as the boat was gently rocking at her moorings, waited as we did for Jeremy. Joan was obviously as nervous as I was.

"Come on, love. Let's look inside." I said to her with a smile.

"Hadn't we better wait until the man comes?" she replied.

THE ADJUTANT WINKED AT ME / Carl Palmer

Not answering I looked around the wheel house at the smart wood planking and the high planked roof which was over our heads. The steering wheel stuck out of the port side and there was a high stool in front of it, with a low railed seat which was obviously the helmsman's perch. To the right of the wheel there was a steel box with a large brown button at the top and the word START printed above it. A brass lever was fitted lower down with a knurled silver button at its base. The lever moved to the left and right around the button obviously and had some function, which was not labelled.

Opening the dark brown thick plywood door in the centre of the boat walls I found steps down into the living section. At the foot of the five steps and to the right (starboard side) was the little shower, handbasin, toilet room, to the left was a similarly small room which was the kitchen (galley) with a radiant fire fitted on the bulk head, a small cooker with two hotplates and a small fridge, a kitchen water basin with hot/cold taps and draining board.

The lounge/living room with collapsible dining table and deeply comfortable couches on either side took up the main part of the room being about eight feet long by six feet wide. A door towards the bow of the boat led to the sleeping quarters, two bunks on the portside above each other and the same on the star board side.

Chapter 5 / THE NORFOLK BROADS

"Hello, there," Can I come in?" this strange musical accent heralded the arrival of Jeremy, whose face appeared above us at the top of the ladder leading to the stern well.

"Hello," we said together, and Joan led the way back as we joined him in the bright ...light which now bathed the stern well of the boat.

"You ever driven a boat like this afore?" said the tall youngster who awaited us standing beside the wheel, with half a smile on his young, unshaven face.

The words of the sentence I have just written are an attempt to convey the sound of the East Anglian accent. "Boat" was more like "boot" and I have taken this trouble because I am sure the speech of this lad in my short helmsman's lesson, did much towards sapping my confidence in the hours that were to follow the five minutes of the lesson.

"No," I emphatically replied, prepared to pay unflinching attention to everything that followed.

"Not to worry. Any fool c'n endle a boat like a this 'n."

Whilst saying this he had turned to the wheel mounting himself on the stool in front of it and pressing the brown button to his right. There was a shudder as the big diesel engine came to life and conversation became a matter of lip reading.

"C'm over 'ere," he beckoned to me. I moved across the boat to stand beside him. Joan had quickly taken a seat on the stern slatted bench holding tightly to the stern rail.

Jeremy shouted "Start, stop button". He pushed the button again and the engine stopped. "You got to remember this nipple as got to be like that when you got the engine off, she's got to be like that, Understand?"

I said, "Yes" but doubtfully.

"I will show you," said Jeremy.

He pointed to the brass lever and its silver button.

"Watch" he pressed the brown button and shudderingly and noisily the engine came to life.

Jeremy left his seat, jumped down the stern ladder, untied the mooring rope and was back beside me in less than half a minute. "You press this 'ere silver nipple in to go forward." He did it and the board moved slightly.

"Then you move this brass lever to the right. Thas throttle".

The boat surged jerkily forward and I stole a look at Joan who was holding on for her life.

Jeremy moved the throttle lever back and I noticed that we were now about forty yards out into the mouth of the river Yare,

"Now," he said "U lissnin?" the boat lost way as he returned the brass throttle lever to … right

Chapter 5 / THE NORFOLK BROADS

"To go astern, you must not move the throttle lever til you pull out the nipple here, "taking the silver knob in his fingers he moved it out, that is towards him., "Then a ... move the throttle to the left which he did and our boat immediately begin to move backwards.

"U got it?" he asked.

"Can you go over it again, a bit more slowly when we're out in the river?" I said.

Obviously unhappy to oblige, something like a snort escaped Jeremy and he said "Old on here then" indicating the wooden arm of the stool he sat on. I hastened to comply.

Pushing the nipple in, he returned the brass lever to the vertical, then he swung the lever quickly to the right so that the engine grunted loudly jerking the boat forward. It was a deliberate act. Thank heaven, he had told me to hold on, or I would have been thrown backward to crash into Joan sitting white-faced on the stern seat. Jeremy knew he had upset me, but I suppressed a hostile reaction. The Yare was about 60 yards wide at this point. Our instructor, I use the word loosely, slowed our speed by gently moving the throttle lever to the right, turned the wheel to starboard, which caused the boat to head slowly to the other side of the river. When we were half way across, Jeremy said, "Watch, then!" he restored the throttle lever to the vertical, so that we lost all speed. "What do I do now?" he said. "Pull out the nipple and gently push the lever to the left," I said.

He made no reply, but did as I had said. The boat moved to the rear, after a flurry of sound from under the stern, turning the bow of the vessel towards the entrance of the boat yard, 50 yards away. "Hold on," he shouted, pushing the nipple in, and we were propelled quickly towards the boat station mooring. Jeremy vaulted over the stern to tie up before returning to join us in the stern well. Before I could ask anything, he said, "Two important things to remember. Yer toilet tanks have to be flushed out once a week, and, she's full of fuel, so you won't have to worry about that. Anyway, there's plenty of gas and water stations along the rivers." He took a scruffy sheet of paper out of his shirt pocket, looked down at it and said. "Oh, yes. Remember to tie up loose every night, the river's tidal, must run engine three hours a day to keep your batteries charged." He jumped on to the bank, and suddenly stopped and looked down at us. With hind sight, I knew he knew he had short-changed us in our instructions. Looking at blank, shell-shocked faces, he said, with an embarrassed smile, and very quietly, so the boss couldn't hear. "You'll be all right." and disappeared.

I was terrified! I looked at Joan, "Don't worry, love. I've got it." I realised I had to put a brave face on

Chapter 5 / THE NORFOLK BROADS

this and get under way while the operating instructions were still in my head. I moved to the stern and released the mooring line, throwing it on to the stern bench with what I hoped, was a nonchalant gesture. I moved to the wheel, pressed the engine start button, and heard the grunt as the big diesel came to life. I made sure the throttle lever was only slightly to the right of vertical, and with a silent prayer, pushed in the nipple. We moved slowly forward and with a thrill, I turned the wheel to starboard to take us out into the River Yare and on our way. I looked over my shoulder at Joan still sitting on the stern seat. She gave me a thin smile, clapped her hands at me for being a clever boy and getting us started after the short handling lesson and came to stand beside me as I pushed the throttle to the right so that our speed was slightly faster. I was struggling to remember all the rules Jeremy had given us and I asked Joan to write them down. "Good idea, love. I'll get a pen from my bag." As she went down into the cabin, I began to cheer up a bit. I pushed the throttle further to the right and though the sound increased, the speed did not noticeably quicken. Then, I remembered that all the cruisers had engine governors fitted as a safety precaution. Looking at the bank to my left, I guessed our speed to a land speed of about 10 mph, but the engine sound was so loud that conversation would be very difficult, so I decreased speed until the decibel count dropped measurably. Joan appeared beside me, putting her arm through mine and immediately, all was once again right with the world.

"Shall I make us a cup of tea, love?" she said. I nodded, and she disappeared into the cabin again. As I carried on, I began to become used to the unchanging scenery at either side of the river. Dense reeds nine to ten feet high bordered the river for as far ahead as I could see. Not a very attractive prospect as far as I was concerned, particularly as I must keep the engine running for three hours a day. Glancing at my watch, I saw it was 2.10 pm, and that meant we had been running for about 40 minutes, so I planned to make my first landing at 3.30 and keep the engine running during our stop.

Joan appeared from the cabin below with my tea. "The engine's awfully loud, love. Can you see if it's quieter if you slow down?" she asked. I moved the throttle lever towards the vertical, but there was a barely perceptible difference in the din. The vibration increased. I pulled a sorry expression to Joan, who frowned as she handed me the tea. She pushed her arm through mine, with a smile and a squeeze which soothed and cheered me up.

"I'm going to look for a place to stop at about half three, love."
"OK, I'm unpacking and finding out about downstairs. Everything's so clean and new; this boat must

Chapter 5 / THE NORFOLK BROADS

have cost a fortune." she said, and disappeared below. It was a super looking boat, with shiny white fibre-glass hull, with gleaming varnished taff-rails and trim along the cabin roof, which was just below eye level as I sat at the wheel. There was a collapsible canopy lying at the stern. There were large bright blue and pear-shaped fenders or shock absorbers hanging at five foot intervals around the vessel to avoid scraping the new paintwork when landing.

The river scenery was monotonous as around every bend it repeated itself; flat land with high reeds bordering the waters edge. Since we had embarked, I had seen no signs of life. Now dead ahead a launch appeared, much like ours, coming up on the far side of the river, the man at the wheel waved and I returned it with what I hoped was a jaunty air. Joan came upon deck, changed into a new pink T shirt, tight white shorts and white deck shoes. Although we had been married for over 20 years I felt a glow of pride at her fresh beauty and glamour. She climbed the steps on the starboard side of the boat and holding tight to the taff-rail stepped towards the bow of the boat. Her petite form was as eye-catching as ever and I was still stirred by the sight of that shapely derriere in her new white shorts. She turned round as if hearing my thoughts, and smiled at me. My heart missed a beat as I smiled back at her, so pleased to see her pleased.

THE ADJUTANT WINKED AT ME / *Carl Palmer*

For some time now we had been passing landing places with mooring posts at twenty yard intervals. The scenery was changing, with moored boats and quaint chalets and cottages at the river side. There were no locks on this stretch of the Yare which was the reason why I had chosen to come this way.

"I'm looking for a stopping place, "I shouted and holding her hand to her ear Joan turned and came back down the boat.

"Couldn't hear you, love"

"I'm going to try a landing. We won't stay long. I just want to see if I can do it. If you go up in the bows, when I tell you, pick up the rope that's there. It's called the painter, then when we've stopped, you jump off and tie the rope around the pole that's there, like I showed you. OK?"

"Right, I'll go back where I was. Just tell me when to jump".

The signs of habitation were thinning again and I began to think we had missed our chance, when I spotted a long stretch of grass with mooring posts about 200 yards ahead of us.

"Jo' look ahead." She turned and nodded. I moved the throttle to the left and was pleased to see our boat lose way at once, as we slowly approached the mooring. When we reached it, I found I had judged it exactly right. Joan was poised as I had told her to be and I shouted. "OK, love jump."

Painter in hand she obeyed the order

Chapter 5 / THE NORFOLK BROADS

Splat! Splat! came the sound as she landed in deep sodden, marshy soil and sank almost up to her ankles in mud! She froze, then turned to look horrified at me as I hurried to jump ashore, but before I could reach her she had tied up to the mooring post as instructed. By the time I had reached her she was struggling to lift her feet from the thick mud which did not wish to cooperate with her. I held out my hand to her as she looked, crestfallen at me. If I had laughed at her, she would have divorced me there and then. She was from a poor home and the ruination of a new pair of shoes however cheap was a serious matter. As I helped her back aboard, I saw the tears in her eyes, and, though she would not have said it for the world, I knew she blamed this disaster entirely on her husband.

When we were on board, I pressed the button to cut the engine as Joan disappeared below to change. I wondered what she would say when she rejoined me. I need not have bothered. "They were only three pounds, love. I don't think I'll be wearing them again" She laughed! I was so proud of her. I should have known she would soon have the thing in its proper perspective. She was smiling at me, "Did I get the knot right?" she said. "Of course you did, love. Otherwise we'd be adrift by now. Well we'd better keep the engine running." I said, and jumping off the boat I hastened to release the bow line, and climbed back aboard. I pressed the engine start button and was pleased to hear the burble at the stern as the engine came to life.

About 25 yards ahead of us was a moored vessel the same size as ours, and as I pressed the start I could see a woman's face peering towards us as she busied herself in the galley. I moved the throttle lever to the right and the engine noise increased as I pulled the wheel to starboard and faced out into the river, but the boat began to drift without any sign of being driven, as it was carried by the current towards the boat next to us. I knew a collision was seconds away as I scrabbled in my mind for what I had done wrong. The woman's face was becoming clearer as I saw her eyes widen at the disaster at hand. "Oh God what can I do?" There were only feet between us when I remembered. "Pull the nipple out for reverse" As I did so, there was a grunt from the engine and immediate response as we moved backwards in to the river, with just a gentle kiss of contact with the neighbouring boat which Joan seemed not to notice. I pushed the nipple back in, turned the wheel to starboard, and we were on our way again.

"Thank you, thank you, God" kept repeating itself in my head, as I pondered my stupidity. I knew that a stupid error of that sort would not recur. "Come on now, enjoy it" I said to myself. With pushing the throttle to the right, our speed

Chapter 5 / THE NORFOLK BROADS

quickened. We knew that all engines had governors fitted which controlled maximum speed to seven knots (about 10 miles per hour). Ahead of us I knew we should enter Breyden water, where the Yare widened to almost a mile and where the river traffic passage was indicated by large poles fixed into the river bed to form a safe lane about 50 yards apart and at 50 yard intervals. At the other side was the fishing port of Great Yarmouth. We turned a long bend in the river and the first of the marker poles came in sight about a half mile ahead. To say I was apprehensive as I approached what seemed to my inexperienced eyes as open sea, is truly an understatement, but I was also thrilled at the prospect of successfully negotiating the trip through the famous East Anglian port ahead of us. At least there was a sense of freedom as we emerged from the narrow river reaches with the boring weed fringes and into open water. As we drew near to the first of the red and white poles, the sun came out and I pushed the throttle lever over to max. There was a perceptible increase in speed, but the noise level grew so much that I pulled back on the throttle and Joan now standing beside me smiled and reading her lips, I saw "That's better, love".

"We should be in the middle of Great Yarmouth soon. I plan to look for a place to stop when we get to the other side of the town. It'll be a relief to

THE ADJUTANT WINKED AT ME / *Carl Palmer*

do without the engine noise for a while, don't you think?" I said.

"Yes, love. I think people should be told about that when they book this sort of holiday. OK, I'll boil some eggs for sandwiches, shall I?" I nodded assent and, giving me a peck on the cheek, she popped into the cabin. I began to enjoy myself with the decreased responsibility of navigation on Breyden water. About 40 minutes later we were getting close to the suburbs of G Yarmouth. I had deliberately slackened speed to almost walking pace, causing far less engine noise and consequently, greater relaxation in my mind. Now we were in the outlying parts of the great sea port and the suburbia from where we could see it was quite up-market. Detached houses with well-kept gardens bordered the river at either side as it narrowed to take us into the densely built town centre. Joan had joined me at the wheel side and had her arm through mine as we came up to the bridge which I guessed to be the centre of town. At either side, protruding from the water were the red and white tide markers so that helmsmen could see whether there was enough water to accommodate their vessel. Our boat needed 10 ft 6 I knew and the markers were showing 16 ft 6, I was relieved to see. People were leaning over the parapet as we approached and we returned their waves as we passed slowly and smoothly under them. My confidence was at last growing after that near disastrous error of forgetfulness at our first landfall.

Chapter 5 / THE NORFOLK BROADS

The river traffic was increasing now. From a line of vessels our side, a very large cruiser pulled out 50 yards ahead of us. It was, I guessed, about 45 feet long and had two decks. I thought it would be a good idea to follow this boat, so tucked in behind her. The name was blazoned across her stern "San Pedro", and I guessed she must have cost £100,000.

"How about a stop for tea soon," Joan said, at my side. "You must be getting hungry, love It's half past four, we must have been going for well over two hours."

"Alright, let's get clear out of Yarmouth, first, then I'll look for a mooring. OK? I feel like something to eat anyway."

I could hear loud music from "San Pedro", which was not to my liking, so I began to look out for our next landing point.

I felt more confident of handling the boat now, and had become used to the constant engine noise. The weather was sunny and I was musing about the reaction of my friends in the pub at home when I told them of my nautical adventures. The only snag about being constantly at the wheel was the sharp draught from the port side chilling my neck and shoulder.

We were now approaching the countryside of the Broads again; boats were less frequent and I began to look for our next stop. There it was, an unoccupied stretch with mooring posts, a couple of hundred yards ahead. I quickly slowed the throttle and shouted for Joan, who appeared almost instantly.

"I'm going to pull in, love," I said and she scrambled along to her place at the bows. "Don't jump off till we stop."

I turned the wheel to port and began to turn the throttle lever to almost stop, but of course we still had quite a bit of momentum. It was not until we were twenty yards away that I saw the vertically planted steel girders, side by side along the whole length of the mooring and, at the same time I realised that I had seriously misjudged my speed, so that our boat, with a horrible grinding sound, scraped for its entire length against the girders in the process cutting two of the beautiful blue fenders adrift. I cut the engine as I saw both of the damaged fenders floating off behind the boat. Joan jumped off the bow and quickly tied up the painter. I stepped off the boat and tied off the stern line. Joan stepped back on board as I with a sinking heart walked along the vessel to assess the damage. Forlornly, I surveyed the scrap of rubber hanging from the ropes where the blue fenders had been and saw that there was a deep scratch in what had, minutes before, been the virginal white of the brand new boat. What was I to do?

Chapter 5 / THE NORFOLK BROADS

When I got back on board, there was the whistling sound of the kettle boiling. I went into the galley to find that Joan had laid out our tea. I said nothing, just looked at her. I was very unhappy because I saw this as a major disaster: obviously and completely my fault. "Don't worry, love. You said yourself, these boats will all be heavily insured." My darling wife said "Now come on. Sit down and eat."

We had not been more than a few hours on the blessed boat and now it was seriously damaged. What dominated my mind was the thought that I would now have to wait to find out whether I would be made to pay for the damage. How could I possibly enjoy the holiday with this on my mind? We looked at each other and I knew Joan was anticipating my reaction, but I still could not speak. She pushed a mug of tea towards me and offered me a sandwich, so I took a bite. If it had been cardboard, it would have tasted the same. I had completely lost my appetite.

"We're going to go back, love" I said. She carried on eating, not looking at me.
"Well I think we haven't given it a fair try." She looked at me with those beautiful big eyes wide open. "You know we won't get our money back, don't you?" She was talking money again; we had different attitudes towards money.

THE ADJUTANT WINKED AT ME / *Carl Palmer*

"And suppose we have another crash." I said. "I just can't stand the responsibility!"

Joan said nothing. She could have said, "I told you so." but she didn't and it made me feel more of a rat.

With everything that had happened, I knew she wanted to go on, and one of the reasons was that she did not want people to think that Carl had failed at something else, but I was really frightened at further disasters. Can you blame me? The silence lasted until she had finished her tea, then she came round the little cabin table to me, put her arm round my neck and said, "OK love. If it makes you happy, then I'm happy too." The memory makes my eyes fill with tears. How did I ever find a woman like that? On this occasion, I made up my mind at once. In the light of the experiences ahead of us, I hope History will not make too harsh a judgment of me.

Joan was quiet now. She had given me the all-clear to abort the trip, so she started to clear up as I decided on our next move. The boring, flat Broads landscape was something I would not miss, anyway. I knew the risks ahead were something I did not want, so, I said, "OK, love Will you come and help me cast off. We're turning her round and going back. We'll have one stop to have a meal, moor for the night, sleep aboard and return the boat tomorrow morning." I looked at her, giving my best smile,

Chapter 5 / THE NORFOLK BROADS

got nothing in return, so snatching my warmest sweater, I made for the deck and the return journey, still apprehensive, but glad to be escaping.

Our mooring was unobstructed by other boats. With luck, I could turn our boat easily and be on our way very quickly. I re-examined our damage as I waited for my wife to join me. The scars along the boats length, the roughly torn remains of the blue fenders, the bitter memory of my incompetence in causing such damage, all reinforced my aborting decision. My heart lifted at the thought of not doing any more harm to this luxury cruiser. We were soon untied fore and aft as I started the engine, watching Joan disappear below, sort of washing her hands of the whole thing, I pushed in the nipple, turned the throttle to the right and made a wide sweep to return in the direction of Great Yarmouth and Cardiff. With some relief, I noticed that the draught was now coming from the other side of the boat so that my sweater would now protect my rapidly stiffening neck.

A large launch much like the San Pedro was about 300 yards ahead of us, so I put on even more speed to come closer to her. My theory was based on the fact that if she got under the bridge at Yarmouth, we should do it easily. I reckoned we were twenty minutes from the bridge which I thought was the only tricky bit to negotiate before we could safely return

THE ADJUTANT WINKED AT ME / *Carl Palmer*

the boat to Reedham. Thank the good God we cannot see into the future! I was slightly concerned that a couple of hours had passed since we had passed through Great Yarmouth, when the water depth marker had shown the depth to give 16 ft of headroom. What would it show as we approached it from this side? I was glad when Joan said, "I'll just go down and start packing."

The boat I was following was pulling away, so I pushed the throttle full ahead. The noise was not tolerable so I eased back, thinking that neither of us could have stood that noise level for long, quietly comforting myself with another reason why I was glad to be aborting the holiday. The eastern suburbs of Yarmouth were coming into sight and I realised that this must be the poor side. Streets of terraced houses appeared and groups of youths playing football close to the waterside stopped to watch us passing. One of them put his hand to his mouth and shouted something to me. I waved back to him. I had only caught one word of his shout, "bridge", but I could make no sense of the rest. I rounded a long bend and was relieved to see the bridge ahead. The big river launch we were following was slowing and as I looked, she slowed pulling sharply to port to a mooring at the busy quayside, obviously the usual mooring, because the manoeuvre was quickly done. Our passage to the bridge was

Chapter 5 / THE NORFOLK BROADS

now unobstructed, but, curiously, it seemed to have sunk in the water.

With a shiver of fear, I saw that the bridge had sunk into their river! I did not recognise it as the bridge we had passed under only hours before. In fact, from the point we had reached, it did not look as though there was any room to pass under it. We were rapidly closing on it, when I decided not to do the sensible thing i.e., to quickly pull over to the port side and look for a mooring, but press on and risk it. I started to feel the panic of sweat on my body as I throttled back and brought us to the centre of the river; Ah, yes! I could see light under the bridge. We would be all right. Even then, I knew I should have stopped. We could both have done with a good night's sleep. If we had stopped then, we may well have decided we could salvage the holiday and carry on to tour the Broads, but, no I was going to press on.

We were about 200 yards from the bridge when I noticed a group of people starting to gather on the parapet of the part of the bridge under which we would pass. I had time to realise that this would be a daily sport for local people disaster-watching. Forty yards from them I could suddenly see the almost submerged tide marker post showing we had 10 ft, and remembered we needed 10ft 6ins! Too late, I was dead centre as we passed under those fiendishly smiling faces and under the bridge. It was OK. I had made it! As I glanced at the underside of the bridge seemingly inches above my head, I saw the big bolt and nut affixed to the bridge dead ahead which we could not possibly avoid, just as we hit it hearing it scrape its length screechingly over my head as we emerged from the other side of the bridge to hear the watching crowd's applause and cheers.

I was shaken, but so grateful to be through and safe, I did not yet want to consider what this latest damage would cost us. I was saying a prayer aloud when I became aware that Joan was standing in the door of the cabin, staring wide-eyed at me.

"What on earth was that scraping noise, and what was the crowd cheering about?" she said.

I said nothing to her, for the moment. I just slumped at the wheel and she came quickly up to me, put her arms around my shoulder and said, "What happened love? You've gone as white as a sheet. Tell me."

Over the next half hour, I explained about the fright I had had when I realised we might not have enough room to pass under the Yarmouth bridge, and then told her of my decision to risk it, of the crowd gathering on the parapet to jeer at us, of how we had nearly made it and then of the projecting bolt which had caused the noise she had heard. By this time I was close to tears and she knew it. No

Chapter 5 / THE NORFOLK BROADS

accusations ensued. She looked at me for a long minute and leaned forward to kiss me and say. "Thank God you decided we should go home, then!" She was still standing with her arm around me as in the near distance I could see the river widening as we approached Breyden water.

"Don't worry anymore, darling. There's nothing much more that can happen to us. Is there? D'you fancy another cup of tea?"

"Please. And plenty of sugar in it." She kissed me quickly on the cheek and disappeared into the cabin. I moved the throttle lever well to the right and the boat surged forward towards home.

As we increased our speed, a really funny thought occurred to me. One of the criteria I apply to every film I see is. Does the action of the film allow any of the characters time to go to the toilet? In this story, I must make it clear that I went to the toilet at our first stop. You will remember. it was when Joan landed in the mud. Now, as I waited for my tea, I became aware of a burning desire "to go", and I wondered whether to cut the engine, so that I could do the necessary.

I must digress here to explain why I hesitated to leave Joan to steer the boat for the few minutes it would take me to relieve myself. Joan could not ride a bike. Whenever you told her something was right, or left she had to look down at her right hand to be able to tell which was the left hand. Giving her simple directions was a long, patience-sapping operation, so the prospect of leaving her in charge of a large cruiser moving over the surface even very slowly was a foolhardiness only a desperate man like me would countenance. Joan appeared beside me and I said, "D'you mind just steering the boat while I go to the loo, love?"

She looked at me wide-eyed, and with a tremor in her voice, said, "OK, love. If you think I can do it. But make it go slower, first. Now what do I have to do?"

"All you have to do is keep us going straight as we are. You see those posts either side of us. "I pointed at the Breyden water marking posts." Just keep us going as we are in the middle of those posts. See I've slowed the boat until we are just doing a walking pace."

There were five or six yachts about a mile on our port side and I did not judge them to be even a slight risk. I held Joan's hands on the wheel and with a quick promise not to be more than minutes, I left her there. I vaulted the steps to the toilet and with huge relief made gushing noises in the toilet. When luxuriating in the emptying of the last water in my bladder, I heard a faint, "Carl," from above my head. Within five seconds, again, "Carl." No

Chapter 5 / THE NORFOLK BROADS

sense of urgency in the call, so I continued best practice to complete my task.

"CAAAAAARL" and I catapulted myself out of the loo and up the steps. A huge white sheet obscured my view. It was a yacht sail. The vessel was directly ahead of us and Joan was steering straight for it. We were no longer than five seconds from cutting the yacht in half. I grabbed the wheel from Joan, pushing her roughly to one side and spun the wheel over to port. I could see the man at the tiller, his eyes wide with terror, as we shaved past his stern and even above the sound of our engine, I heard, and will never forget the word "BASTARD" echoing across Breyden water.

Joan had fallen over as I corrected our left turn and brought us back on course. "Sorry, love" I said, covering my own panic. I am quite sure she was blissfully unaware of the tragedy we had narrowly averted.

"Well you said I was to keep on going straight, so I knew I should not turn the wheel." she looked at me with quizzing eyebrows. To have attempted to explain would not have worked, so I just smiled and throttled up. Gazing in the wake of our near victim, I was relieved to find he was almost out of sight, a mile to our starboard. Through my head a chorus of "thanks to God prayers" was continually transmitted as I tried to take stock of the sheer numbers of disastrous incidents we had lived through that day. I could hardly believe what we had been through. Surely no one had experienced so many close shaves in one day. As we covered the great expanse of Breyden water, my most earnest prayer was that nothing else would happen to us so that the boat could be safely returned in the next day. Please, please GOD. I took great pleasure in the correctness of the decision I had taken to abort this holiday ... almost preened myself on it!!

On the banks of the Yare at the western end of Breyden water is a pub called The Berney Arms. I had chosen this as our last mooring today. It was approaching 7.00 pm, so I intended to tie up and have dinner together there. Dusk was fast gathering as leaving Breyden behind us we cruised into the narrowing Yare and soon sighted a long stone Quayside with Berney Arms sign neon illuminated at either end. The pub was to be our first real landfall and, tired and drained as we both were, we couldn't wait to be refreshed and relieved of our responsibilities for a while. I turned across the river to coast up to a clearly marked mooring fifty yards to the west of the inn. Joan had already moved into the bows with a painter in her hand, and I approached the bank very slowly, so all she had to do was to step down off the boat and tie up to a post on the clean, grey-stone surface of the quay. Cutting the engine, I jumped off and tied off the stern rope. I was greatly

Chapter 5 / THE NORFOLK BROADS

relieved and noticed a sharp appetite for meal at the Berney Arms. As we washed, changed and prepared, the huge relief of the absence of engine noise helped to allay the worries I felt over all that had happened to us, but the overall feeling of joy at the imminent shedding of responsibility for the boat was the single factor that gave me most pleasure.

As I strove to think of the avoidance of any more frights before tomorrow's handover, I remembered the sentence, "Remember it's a tidal area, so telling Joan I was just popping up to check our moorings, I stepped down on to the quay and saw that the ropes were rather tight. Untying both , I retied them giving almost three feet of slack in each, proud of myself for my expertise, I saw that Joan had been watching and now handed her down off the boat looking very glamorous in white slacks and a bright red sweater. Hand in hand we walked to the pub together.

There were a few people eating at the large restaurant, so having been taken to a table, I left Joan menu-browsing and went to the bar for drinks. There was a middle-aged customer sitting on a bar-stool who suddenly leaned back hooting with laughter as the landlord continued with his story.

"He just left the boat moored 'ere at number 7, with half the cabin 'anging off and gave me the keys. He and 'is missus just walked across the fields to catch the bus to Reedham Grange and get a train 'ome, said 'eed phoned the yard at Reedham. I've 'ad enough, he said" The customer on the bar-stool was now speechless with mirth.

"Sorry to keep you waiting, Sir" he said. "How can I help you?"

"Two gin and tonics, please. What happened, then?" I asked.

"Old gent, came in 'ere last night at about this time; misjudged the tide at Great Yarmouth, caught the roof of his cabin against the bridge, nearly ripped 'n off. Not the worst I've heard, mind. Bloke last month got 'is boat stuck under the bridge; the river police had to get him out, could have been nasty. Two pound eighty, please.".

I walked back to Joan trembling inside, but truly grateful we were on the way home. I decided not to tell Joan about what I'd heard; I would keep it for the journey home.

"I've ordered you a well-done sirloin, love. Is that all right?" She said "Fine," I put the drink down.

"I hope the man in the yacht doesn't report us. But, at least, we didn't hit him."

As I took a swig at the lovely G and T, I pondered the scene that could have resulted if I had arrived 10 seconds later from the toilet; the yacht in pieces and the gurgling sound as our holed launch began its descent into the depths of Breyden water.

"You can still change your mind, love. We don't have to go home tomorrow." Joan said.

Chapter 5 / THE NORFOLK BROADS

"No, it's too much of a responsibility. Not only that, the noise factor is beginning to get me down." I smiled at her persistence. She looked at me, raising her eyebrows, making it plain that she wanted me to know the responsibility for cancelling the holiday was entirely mine. We dropped the subject.

The steaks were good. We had two or three more drinks, and, by then, the memory of some of the drama of the day had blurred. We strolled arm in arm back to the boat, neither of us noticing that we stepped down on to the deck of our boat. I remember thinking how lucky it was that we had been running so long, because the boat's lights were brilliant when I switched them on. The drinks we had consumed had worked well in blurring the edges and as soon as we undressed for bed, after a brief goodnight kiss, we were both soon asleep.

I woke in an extended dream of strange sounds and a sense of a swinging motion. The sound was of a creaking and the motion was very noticeable. At the end of each swing, the movement seemed to turn in the opposite direction, ending in a jarring sensation as the collision bumped quite loudly. I have forgotten how long I endured this until the inevitable happened.

"What is it, love?" Joan said. I peered through the darkness, and could make out her lovely face caught in a sliver of moonlight momentarily. "You'll have to go out and see, love"

"OK. I won't be a minute, you stay there"

I slipped out of bed and got to my feet, just as the in-swing started. I became scared as I nearly lost my balance. Grabbing a hat I put my duffel on and gingerly climbed the four steps to the door to the stern well. I hid my fear as best I could. Opening the door, I stared up at a rainy sky.

For a moment, I could not believe my eyes. Standing in the cabin doorway, still on the fourth step leading to the stern well, I looked up at the bank topped by the wall of the quayside over the edge of which our mooring line disappeared. The rope's tautness was indicated by the drops of water springing from it as we swung slowly in and out from the bank. Very gingerly I stepped out so that I could see the line from the bows. Just as I turned to look, the boat bumped against the bank and I almost lost my balance. The painter, looking ridiculously thin, was taut as the stern line, and standing with fear in my heart for a moment I was paralysed at the thought of what I would find when I looked over the side of the boat, but I had to look. Moving gently, I put one of my hands on the gunwale and peered over the side. We were suspended against the quayside. The black surface of the river was at least 10 feet below the keel. I froze inside as I realised we were dependant on those two mooring ropes for our lives.

Chapter 5 / THE NORFOLK BROADS

"Carl, are you all right, love?" Joan called from the cabin behind me.

"Please Lord let the ropes not break" I whispered.

Forcing a relaxed smile to my face, I carefully stepped down into the cabin again.

"It's lucky I tied the mooring loosely." I said. "The tide is coming in fast, so the boat will soon steady herself again." Joan looked at me dubiously. "How about some tea and toast, love?" She immediately went into the galley to get our breakfast. Within ten minutes we were sitting together having our meal, cosily warmed by the electric wall fire. "I'll write about this one day. Trouble is nobody will believe so much happened in one day," Joan did not laugh, but picked up our plates and went out to wash them.

There was nothing we could do but wait, so I started to pack my bags. I had not been long at it when I heard the lapping of water under the boat. I said a silent and heartfelt prayer, and just a short while later, the lapping noises stopped and the boat was afloat again. I stepped out on deck to verify what I had heard. Dawn was already up. The gunwales of our boat were only about three feet below the level of the quay. We were safe! I had one of those bursting feelings of happiness a new day can bring, and sent up a stream of hymns of thanksgiving. There was a gorgeous smell of bacon coming from the galley, and, surely enough, Joan's cheerful shout of "Grub up!" About an hour later, I started up the engine and we began our slow and stately cruise back to the Reedham boatyard. Musing on our way of whether our chapter of misfortunes would have been significantly less if our instruction period had been properly conducted. Of course it would!

When we arrived at the boat yard, I carefully docked at the pontoon from which we had left and, luckily for us, Mr. Hampson was there standing at our landing stage pulling a comically quizzical expression. I quickly tied up, jumped ashore and told him how we had lost the blue fenders. He did not turn a hair. "Don't worry about that. We'll replace them in a jiffy," he said, "Then you can be on your way again!"

He was so cooperative, that I reached the conclusion that this sort of interview was far from unusual to him. When he said he would refund our forty pounds fuel charge as we were handing the boat back to him, I was pleased at his great generosity. He then apologized that he could refund us nothing for the boat but promised us a half-price cruise at any time in the future, I was truly amazed. Thirty years later, I am still not tempted to accept his offer!!!

6

UNFORGETTABLE MEMORIES

A lifetime spent as a full-time teacher has had its share of laughs. I believe that a teacher who has not a healthy sense of humour is in the wrong job. In the year I began teaching, 1964, one of the classes I taught (I use the term, lightly) was 4d. The initial in the name of this class gives a good clue to their intelligence level. The school was a Secondary Modern, pupilled by eleven year olds who had failed the infamous 11+ and Elementary English was the subject. I tried to teach writing in sentences, spelling, simple grammar, writing letters both the personal and business variety: at the end of the week, we also had reading lessons. If they had been very good all week, we might have a Drama lesson. Anything that would hold their attention was acceptable. I also took them for one Geography lesson per week. I would try to provide interesting pictures to make the dry study which the syllabus directed acquire flesh and bones, and therefore be more attractive to them.

It was towards the end of my second term when examinations were due to take place on a Friday morning. I had told the class that their paper would contain twenty questions. With children of limited ability short answers were necessary. Simple instructions were essential, so that those people who had revised well might score top marks. The atmosphere was electric and tense as I gave out the papers.

"Please put your name and form at the top of the paper." I said. As I walked around with the papers, I saw Emrys at the back had his hand up.

"What is it, Emrys?" I said.

"Sir, have we got to write our name and form at the top of the paper?" he said.

There was a buzz of interest. "Stop talking and listen to me. Are you all listening, everybody? Everyone put your name and form on the top of your paper. All right, Emrys?"

Emrys smiled and nodded.

"I am going to write the questions on the board. As soon as I have done that, I will turn the board round so you can see it. You must then answer all the questions, right?"

Chapter 6 / UNFORGETTABLE MEMORIES

The blackboard was free standing with squeaky wheels so I turned it away from them and towards me and began writing. The writing of the questions did not take long, so I put up with the buzz of voices. I had included two silly questions to make them laugh. Question 3, Name the country from which we get Brazil nuts. And Question 7, Write down the name of the country that grows Brussels sprouts.

When I had finished, I stood with my hand on the side of the board ready to turn it round.
"Put your books away. If I see anyone looking to the side, or talking, I will cancel his paper."
I turned the board and watched them; waiting for someone to spot the silly questions and react …. There was not a sound. Everyone was busy writing. No one got all the answers right!

The final exam in History by the pupils nationally, was called The Certificate of Merit. The Welsh version of this exam covered the various syllabuses used by all Welsh schools; therefore the paper contained eighty questions. The rubric was clear, "Candidates must answer ONE question from Section A, and any four questions from the rest of the paper, making a total of FIVE questions.

In my School, the Invigilator read the instructions with great care, pointing out that everyone

THE ADJUTANT WINKED AT ME / *Carl Palmer*

should only answer five questions. The paper was of two hours duration. Having seen my candidates start, I left, returning 20minutes before the exam ended. When I entered the exam room, I noticed that the majority of candidates had finished. One or two were still writing, but I had to look severely at the rest and, with gestures, indicate that they should turn around in their seats and re-check their answers. Emrys, when I sat down, rose from his seat looking worried, came out to my desk and took another sheet of paper, hurrying back to his seat. Fifteen minutes later, other members of staff arrived to help me close down the exam.

"Right, put your papers and pens down. The examination is finished." I said. My colleagues and I passed among the desks collecting papers. Emrys was still writing, his forehead creased, he was making strange, impatient clucking noises.

"Come on, Em." I said, tiredly. "Let's have your papers."

Unhappy and red-faced he looked up at me.

"Orright, Sir. You can have my papers, but I 'aven't finished. I'm only up to number sixty four."!!!!

Throughout my teaching life, I was never one to miss morning assembly. It was always my personal belief that assembly was important not only for its religious purpose, though that should always be carefully planned in these days of "multi-faith", but so that the pupils saw that teachers were there

Chapter 6 / UNFORGETTABLE MEMORIES

too and for the reason that growing humans take great comfort from being part of a great crowd in common endeavour.

One Head teacher I knew provided (accidentally) the funniest moment I have ever witnessed at assembly. It was the last day of a winter term in the seventies, and Mr. P decided he would address the entire senior school. With this in mind, he announced in a staff meeting that he expected all available staff to attend Christmas assembly. With hind sight, it was just as well that he had done this, because the increased number of teachers present was a factor that saved the day.

This man had a particular talent for choosing words and expressions that could be taken the wrong way, I'm sure the reader will remember that school children are quick to spot the " double-entendre". There was the infamous occasion when this same Head in describing the huge feat of bravery of a well-known cross-channel swimmer declared to his friends afterwards that he attributed his survival to his little lucky charm which he always carried tucked into his swimming trunks (this pointed further by a gesture by the Head towards his own nether regions) The explosion of suppressed laughter took the combined efforts of the staff to bring under control.

THE ADJUTANT WINKED AT ME / Carl Palmer

On this Christmas occasion, elation at the thought of escape was spreading its goodwill as we waited to hear what pearls would be shared this year. The obligatory, "While shepherds watched ....." preceded the Head's speech, then some tiresome announcements, then the hostile threats not to dare to set off the fire alarms under penalty of expulsion if caught.

Finally, with a hitch of his gown up around his shoulders, the Head began his address. The microphone worked well and the kids, all five hundred of them listened attentively. It was a sensible topic, the purpose of generosity at Christmas, The Head had prepared carefully and we, his colleagues smiled with pride in being associated with him. He talked of how proud he was of the pupils who donated with real enthusiasm to the "fill a shoe box for Bosnia "scheme. He complimented the school choir on their brilliant concerts, the proceeds of which were being sent to, "Crisis at Christmas " and the children warmed to his sincerity. He obviously sensed this and began to play to the gallery as all public performers do when they feel the audience is with them. The trouble with such a practice is that the speaker abandons his planned words and wanders in uncharted waters.

The Head then told us of the family customs in his own home; of how his children still liked to hang

Chapter 6 / UNFORGETTABLE MEMORIES

up their Christmas stockings, although they were now grown-ups. Smiles and sympathetic murmurs here told him he still had them in the palms of his hands. His wife, he told us always gave him lovely presents on Christmas morning: a moments pause here, perfectly judged, as he came to the point, "But, remember, boys and girls, it is always better to give than to receive. I always like to give my wife one, before we get up on Christmas morning!"

If a mortar bomb had exploded in the hall, it could not have made more noise. Someone said later, they heard the Head say, "I meant a present." as he stood there in front of the laughter, his gown flapping wildly, his face bright red, as we moved amongst the kids slowly quitening them after the hilarious confession of the Headmaster.

"Corpsing" is a term well known to the theatrical profession. It occurs when something is said, or happens during the performance of a play which is completely unexpected, and effectively "kills" the character concerned. Sometimes this is accidental, for example, a person about to make an exit through a door off stage finds that the door handle comes off in his hand, or that the door is jammed: this, not only corpses the person concerned, but also, anyone else on stage at the time. Sometimes mischievous actors may engineer a situation designed to corpse a fellow actor.

THE ADJUTANT WINKED AT ME / *Carl Palmer*

I remember playing a small part in "Billy Liar" for the Cardiff Little Theatre in my youth, Stanley, Billy's father would enter, carefully take off his hat and coat to hang them on a door hook, then, with a line of greeting to his wife, begin to eat a meal which his wife would place there for him. The meal was the same every night, cold ham, fried potatoes and a large whole tomato, The actor had said, several times during the week's run how much he enjoyed eating the meal, and we had all said how much we envied him.

On the Saturday evening, we had replaced Stanley's meal with plastic display ham, tomato (large) and fried potato, and we had positioned ourselves in the wings to see his reaction. He entered from up right, hung his coat and hat up, kissed his wife and sat at the table, immediately taking his knife and fork in his hands; he drew the knife across the ham slice. For a fraction of a second he glared at the plate, then looked straight at us, convulsed in the wings. His face was red, and then he tried, none too gently to plunge the fork into the juicy, red tomato, which promptly tried to leave the scene! It was his quick reflexes which enabled him to catch the tomato in mid-flight and return it to his plate.

Chapter 6 / UNFORGETTABLE MEMORIES

The actor playing Stanley was a senior Coal Board official in real life, so that his quick wits saved him. He had soon spotted that the bread and butter was real and casually he made a meal of that, to which we responded from the wings with a silent round of applause. I will leave it to the reader's imagination to dwell on what Stanley said to the planners of his downfall during the interval.

Sometimes a corpsing scene which does not go according to plan can wreak havoc. The following is a true story of the telling of a joke, it's not the joke that is so funny, but the circumstances in which it was told, but, most of all, who told it. Swansea, in the 1950s was closer to the Bible belt than was Cardiff, therefore it was usual to meet the strait-laced attitude: this is a leading feature in this story of a massive "corpsing" in which I became a guilty party.

The play was "The Atom Doctor" by Eric Linklater, a long-winded, slow to develop and easy to forget plot with quite a large cast. I will, however, always remember the central character in this tale. Her name was Tegwen (equal stress on both syllables, please.). She was a nursing sister in a local hospital, serious and quiet-spoken. She was obviously taking Drama to give her more confidence in herself. She was a short-haired brunette, well-built,

THE ADJUTANT WINKED AT ME / *Carl Palmer*

but not a waster of words whom no one in the cast knew well.

In Act 3, the leading man, Dr Mortimer has a scene down stage right which is very important to the plot, in which he says something vital to the female lead. On stage at the time is a group of characters, of which I am one, whom the director has placed up-stage left around a table making after-dinner small talk. The Director told us, "Look, you lot, I can't have you all standing there doing nothing. I suggest it would be a good idea to take it in turns to tell a joke at this point, every night. A little tittering from you lot will not disturb the action and look much more natural. OK?"

We all agreed, it was a good idea, to be strictly truthful. We did not all agree. Tegwen openly told us all she was very unhappy about it. "I don't know any jokes." she said. A few wry smiles amongst us, spoke volumes! We would have been amazed if she had. But, the Director's idea worked remarkably well. Every night in Act Three we took it in turns to tell a mildly funny story and the gentle laughs that resulted, eased the serious business downstage to take place realistically. It was to be the turn for Tegwen's joke on the Saturday and she had told me privately she was dreading it. I said, "Don't worry, Teg. You'll be all right!"

Chapter 6 / UNFORGETTABLE MEMORIES

The curtain opened on a full house on the Saturday night, a packed house is always a joy to actors, and we were soon enjoying the performance. Act three opened and towards the end Dr Mortimer took the young leading lady to have their important conversation. We five were in position around the table. Nothing was said, so I prompted Tegwen, "Right, Teg, it's your turn." We all looked expectantly at her, she hesitated for a second, looked dubiously round at us and began.

"This lady went into Timothy Whites and Taylor, the chemist and said to the assistant. Excuse me, but do you sell chamber pots?"

"No, said the assistant. Have you tried "BOOTS"

"Yes, said the lady, but it comes out of the lace holes."

Ann, who was standing next to Teg, shrieked a laugh, putting her hand to her mouth, trying in vain to stifle it. I laughed aloud, and Bernard nearly choked and went red in the face in his efforts to prevent exploding. Old Jim, the seasoned veteran amongst our group, with his hand to his face, had taken his handkerchief out and was giggling behind it. More to the point, the audience were laughing by now. Dr Mortimer and his interlocutor might as well have died, because that's what had happened to the play.

THE ADJUTANT WINKED AT ME / Carl Palmer

I can never call that silly joke to mind without actually laughing. Tegwen, who was only doing as she had been told had corpsed the whole performance. I learned something very important: never use that device. Remember it's not the joke, that's funny, it's the teller.

One of the plays I produced was "Smike", a musical version of the Dickens character's life as a pupil at the infamous Do the boys Hall in Yorkshire. In the frenzied first run of the dress rehearsal on a Saturday afternoon, everything was going wrong. The set was poorly lit, lots of the props still had to be found, and the little outdoor fire I had asked for, as the latest crop of pupils waited in the cold under the eagle eye of Wackford Squeers, had still not appeared.

I was giving notes during a short break before the final dress rehearsal. The stage manager, a lovely, sensible senior girl was the aim of my tongue lashing. She was being "helped" in the wings, by other sixth-formers, and I suspected horseplay.

"Now, Val, you will agree, I hope that things are not going well."

"Yes, Sir. " was the reply.

"I'm glad of that, by the way, what silly fool hung that red bra over the arm of that chair down stage?" I barked, glaring at her.

Chapter 6 / UNFORGETTABLE MEMORIES

She bridled, put her hands on her hips and said, "You said you wanted a brassiere near the chair, Sir. There was nowhere else I could put it!"

I took her to one side and apologized, explaining the reason I had been cross. We laughed together and later she found a real brazier in which she hid a bulb behind some crepe paper, the problem was solved.

In my mid-forties I taught a Drama class for the WEA, Workers Educational Assoc., on a Friday evening, 6.30-9.30pm. Can you imagine the strain of teaching a class in which the average age was mid sixties, and at the end of a working week with screaming kids? Suffice it to say, it was very hard to stay motivated.

For Easter, we chose to stage some excerpts from the Coventry Mystery play cycle. Most of the members were practising Christians, and the premises under which we had our existence was Charles Street Congregational Church. To be fair, the standard of performance the group achieved was usually good, though one of the exasperating facts was the length of time it took them to learn their lines, but, by the time the opening night arrived, they were always word perfect. The difficulty arose when I asked an older married couple, Jack and Minny (already married 56years!) to play two angels, one of whom had to speak a line as they stood in the garden on Resurrection morning.

Of course, neither of them wanted to speak the line; so, unselfishly, Minny decided it would be Jack. Jack made it very plain that he was against the idea from the start, but, as he put it "orders is orders". Now, Jack was a retired steel worker, and it is not doing him a disservice to say that he was not a cultured person, neither was he very refined. In the play he and his wife were required to stand either side of the up-stage area and Jack, on cue would speak the line, " Hie thee hither in haste." to Mary, mother of God and the apostle, John, Jack would also point upstage in the direction of the tomb.

Jack hated the responsibility and almost weekly, tried in vain to wriggle out of it. I know the line was difficult to say, with hind-sight I realised I should have changed it .I cannot recall Jack ever getting the line completely right: we heard, "i.e. thee 'ither in Haste" or some other variation, but he just could not get all the aitches in order. All the rehearsals came to the point of Jack's line and afforded endless amusement to the rest of the cast, doing their best to hide their smiles.

At this point, I must make it plain that this venerable couple, Jack and Milly were elders in the Church in which they were about to make their

Chapter 6 / UNFORGETTABLE MEMORIES

acting debut. The church was packed on Maundy Thursday eve, and we were all excited. Please remember, congregationalists are a strait-laced sect.

The play would last about an hour including a ten minute interval. In the dressing room, I could see Jack deep in thought as Minny helped him to put on his carefully ironed and snow-white serplice which was a copy of the one she was wearing. She was obviously light-hearted about the performance not having to worry about speaking any lines and my heart went out to her poor and very anxious husband.

The play went well and in the interval, as we could hear the buzzing and excited audience making complimentary comments about our play, I told them how proud I was of them glancing towards Jack, but I could see he was not reachable because of his anxiety. The next scene was Jack and Minny's, so I gave them both the thumbs up sign as they took their places on stage.

When I took up my place just hidden behind the return wall no more than two feet from Jack's ear, I prayed fervently that he would manage to deliver the line on cue. I was following the script carefully, my heart in my mouth as his cue line was spoken. Nothing. Nothing. Nothing.

"Jack," I whispered."Hie thee hither....."

THE ADJUTANT WINKED AT ME / *Carl Palmer*

"Hie thee Hither in 'aste!" Jack shouted. Then, completely forgetting his gesture to Mary and John, who were looking expectantly in his direction, he walked off upstage muttering in what he thought was inaudible," Oh Christ, never again! " I stole a peep round the return wall at the audience and from their red faces and hands in front of their mouths, I could see they were as amused as I was and I have no doubt at all that The God who witnessed the torment of Jack was laughing as much as we were.

I became a magistrate in my late thirties, and when a few years had passed I was on the bench, fortunately still a winger on a bench of three, at a "lock-up" court, that is a court which handles urgent overnight matters. Serious crimes as well as trifling matters are dealt with by the bench. Such a court is always filled with police and lawyers eager to have their cases heard.

On the morning in question, I was sitting with an experienced Chairman (who was a woman), and another winger. Shop-lifters, drunks, juveniles, Bail applications by the dozen soon occupied us. There was also a number of prostitutes!

It was the calling of the name of one of these ladies of the night, that suddenly drew my attention. "Call Jane Davies. Jane Davies, Jane Davies!"

Chapter 6 / UNFORGETTABLE MEMORIES

I had not checked the court list before coming in to court. I looked at the young lady approaching the dock and hastily leaned forward and touched the clerk's shoulder. He turned round immediately.

"I taught this girl." I said

He could not hide his smile, as I hastily added, I mean in school" and blushed furiously.

"That's alright, Mr Palmer," He smiled his delight at me. "Just move your chair to the right: to show you are not adjudicating."

The solid, hardwood chairs of the period could not be moved inconspicuously, so as I stood to move mine, I heard a chorus of sniggering giggles from the packed benches in front of me

At this point, Jane realised that she knew one of the magistrates.

"OO hello , Mr Palmer!"

Much snuffling, choked laughter, and delighted expressions from the advocates benches ensued.

"How do you plead?" hooted the clerk.

"Oh sorry, " said my ex-pupil. "Guilty."

I will never forget how guilty I felt that day, as Jane continued to smile at me as the police evidence was read out and I felt voyeuristic as I had to listen to embarrassing evidence.

"We are retiring to read the Social inquiry reports." announced the Chairman

"All stand," said the clerk, as I rose to my feet with my two colleagues.

"Not you, Mr Palmer!" said the clerk

Once again suppressed titters from the audience. My colleagues retired and I was left to the mercy of the waiting lawyers and, of course, to the defendant Jane, who smiled without the slightest embarrassment. I responded by looking away quickly.

Fortunately, the court resumed within ten minutes.

The chairman had reached the decision with which I heartily agreed by mildly reproving Jane and giving her a Conditional discharge. Almost certainly agreeing with the recommendation of the social enquiry report.

I think now, and thought then, how ludicrously unfair it is to penalise only the female half in such incidents.

On this occasion, I began to think I had escaped as Jane left the dock, but suddenly she thought better of it. She turned and said in a loud voice, "Thank you very much, Mr Palmer. It's lovely to see you again."

Barely muffled chuckles from my audience, who probably dined out on that incident for the next few weeks.

I remember a performance of the Wakefield Mystery in Llandaff Cathedral when I was in my thirties. I had been cast as Judas Iscariot. It was professionally produced with a huge cast, well-known professional actors were in the leading roles and as the production matured, it became plain that it was

Chapter 6 / UNFORGETTABLE MEMORIES

to be a memorable show. The sad thing was that it would be a single performance as it was slotted into the Llandaff Festival.

I must explain that a stage was built about six feet high underneath the Majestas, an Epstein Christ standing between the nave and the chancel. A huge golden and arching staircase led to God's throne, 15ft above the stage. The production was perfectly in tune by the time we opened. Anyone who has ever seen a play of this sort will know how powerful the images created can be and, also how the old English gives a strong validity to the well-known lines from the Bible.

My scene of the betraying kiss to Jesus was well rehearsed and tellingly staged and when I was preparing to go on, in front of 800 other human beings and hiding behind the isolating power of thousands of kilowatts of light, I found I was shaking with the experience. I felt as Judas must have felt – reluctant but impelled towards a terrible betrayal. The expectant silence of the audience as I walked towards Jesus, put my hands on his shoulders and delivered the most famous betraying kiss in dramatic history, is something I will never forget. I still shiver in the realism created and the shame I felt. For me, it was a Road to Damascus experience, never since have I come as close to knowing the

THE ADJUTANT WINKED AT ME / *Carl Palmer*

presence of God in my life and the healing power of repentance and absolution.

This is undoubtedly one of the most unforgettable of my experiences. Looking back on that memorable production to try to understand why I felt as I did is now easy for me to explain. Particularly in the light of the way I spend my life forty years on as a Lay Chaplain in the hospital service. Most days I am involved in praying for or with patients, so the power of prayer has become a regular experience to me. Llandaff Cathedral has been hearing prayers for centuries , so it is not at all difficult for me to believe that I actually betrayed Jesus in the person of Judas on that night forty years ago . At the end of all the Mystery plays the wicked souls are harried down to hell, and on the night I refer to, I remember feeling as guilty as Judas must have as I joined the shrieking crowd as we howled on reaching hell, all damned to eternity forty years ago.

Thank the goodness of God it was only a play!

7

PARTING, PROZAC AND PRAYERS

Joan decided to become a teacher when she was almost forty. Her Grammar school results were much better than mine, so there was no trouble enrolling in the College of Education as a mature student, and she chose to study English and Drama, as I had. Her progress was rapid as a student. I had always believed that she was much brighter than I, and she was soon providing the evidence. She made student friends easily, and among the college staff there were people we knew, which made her integration into the course flow smoothly and enjoyably for her. She found too, that her rather severe public manner was perfectly suited to the air of authority that is an asset when faced with a crowd of youngsters.

THE ADJUTANT WINKED AT ME / *Carl Palmer*

She thoroughly relished her student days, and in no time had reached the end of the course and the final teaching practice at Our Lady's Convent, a private RC girls' school. During the teaching practice, the staff were impressed with Joan's conscientious work and easy manner with girls of all ages. They were so pleased with her that the Head, a Sister Mary Angela, offered her a part-time post before the end of her teaching practice. The exam results brought confirmation of her ability as well as practice as a teacher, and she was invited to stay an extra year which meant she could graduate as a Bachelor of Education.

She was, of course, tempted to stay, but the offer from the Convent was "a bird in the hand". She asked my advice and I made it clear that whatever she decided was OK with me. Taking a long time to decide (typical of her) she opted to take the offer from the Convent and started teaching three days a week in September 1974.

By this time, I had been teaching for ten years and had a Head of Department allowance for Drama, so that our joint salaries gave us a new prosperity. It was lovely to see Joan opening up like a flower. After her other working life of deadly dullness in the bank, she now discovered she could wield her knowledge expertly in teaching youngsters. Her

Chapter 7 / PARTING, PROZAC AND PRAYERS

genuineness as a mature woman, her glamorous appearance, her strong character and acting flair soon won her acclaim amongst and a place in the hearts of young people.

Although she had sacrificed the B Ed., course, she was soon studying with the OU for an Arts degree, this on top of caring for me with the array of household tasks that that involved. It was a happy time for us as her frustration at the age of sixteen in being denied the university education for which she was so obviously suited, could now be remedied in the comfortable circumstances we now enjoyed.

The staff at the Convent soon realised they had acquired a valuable friend and hard-working colleague. Joan had a visible integrity and sincere manner which quickly established her place on the staff of this prestigious private school. All her teaching friends liked and respected her, and she had a very happy life as a teacher.

In the field of Child Drama she became a producer of school plays which were highly lauded. Her production of "Smike", a musical play based on the life of a Dickens character from "Nicholas Nickleby", was highly praised and stressed Joan's other talent as a person with theatre ability. That period in her life was a delight to her as it opened up new avenues in her life in which she was able to shine.

Physically, Joan was a small person and her weight, even when soaking wet and pregnant never reached much above eight stone. In the later years of our marriage, I began to share more of the household chores. It would be a complete lie to state that I did more than a small fraction. Joan worked like a steam engine at whatever she applied herself to, and it was only when she was gone that I realised how essential she was to the life-style we enjoyed as the kids grew up and left us in later years.

Early in 1978, Joan developed a strange illness, both an eating disorder and debilitating complaint, so that she suffered serious weight loss and extreme tiredness. Her work load was considerable, and in the late seventies, because of my mother's death we had an extension built, so that my father could come to live with us. Although he was eighty two and fairly fit, he was handicapped by increasingly poor sight and this extra mouth to feed was almost the last straw to Joan's work load. She had resisted from the first, to having my dad to live, but eventually gave in. My daughters were teen-age and sensitive, so that another man to care for strained Joan to breaking point. Her disease was diagnosed as Crohn's, and after a hospital stay, she improved enough to carry on not only as housewife and carer

Chapter 7 / PARTING, PROZAC AND PRAYERS

daughter-in-law, but went back to full-time teaching. She also enrolled to do "Honours" in the OU. With hind-sight, I am convinced that this colossal commitment had caused the Crohn's.

However, dad became more of a part of our daily round, to a large extent due to Joan's unstinting care and kindness towards him. They had become firm friends from their first meeting and in the days when we were young marrieds, and money was tight, my dad would always help out when we were in need. I well remember finding Joan in tears when I came home one day. She had opened our bank statement and found we were eleven pounds overdrawn in the current account. As a previous bank clerk, this was a shame too great to bear. A phone call to dad resulted in an immediate visit with cheque to save her face and ensure friendship for life.

Crohn's had taken the stuffing out of Joan, but not damaged her love of teaching. Her last personal stage performance, for she was eagerly sought after by AMDRAM companies in Cardiff, was to play the mother in John Mortimer's "A Voyage Round My Father" in the Sherman Theatre. She was acclaimed for a beautifully judged characterization. It taxed her, though, and she said to me after the run ended, "It's not worth the effort, love. It takes too much time for rehearsal and in nervous energy. I will never do that again." Her final performance was much praised, but, sad to say, she never acted again.

By the mid nineteen-eighties, our younger daughter, Catrin had gone to college in Middlesex, so Joan, Dad and I were on our own in the reasonably large family home. With our commitments to schools and my frequent rehearsals, my father was left on his own all day. We would meet at tea time to eat together, after which, Dad would return to his upstairs flat and we would spend the evenings together, after we had each done any marking, or lesson prep, a time we cherished.

It was after dinner early in March 87, that we met the first sign of Joan's final illness. She had been lying on her right side on a couch in our living room for a much needed nap. I thought she was making funny breathing noises, and when she woke, she spoke hoarsely and needed to get to her feet to cough and clear her throat. She was still busy at the OU study I have mentioned earlier.

The symptoms recurred regularly so she saw our GP who assured her it was nothing to worry about, I wonder how many times that evasion has been successful. A referral for X ray followed and when nothing happened for a couple of months, we were reassured through the casual turning of NHS wheels that this was a good sign.

Chapter 7 / PARTING, PROZAC AND PRAYERS

About mid-summer, when school had ended, Joan attended the Heath hospital for X ray with a follow up appointment with the GP, who told her that there was something in the thorax which the hospital would like to investigate further, but there was nothing urgent about it. Joan told him about her final OU exam scheduled for mid October, so he agreed that the next appointment would be for an investigative procedure in Llandough at the end of October. We were still not alarmed.

Summer proceeded: that essential oasis in every teacher's life when sanity is restored. There was no worsening of Joan's symptoms, so we had a good break and returned to school in September. Joan's time was taken up by striving for the "Honours" endorsement to her BA. We both prepared for her hospital date which had been set for October 20th. Two days before this, she visited Llandough hospital for tests and was told to expect a short stay because she was to have a surgical procedure. On the 20th, I drove her to the hospital, about five miles from our home where I waited and brought her clothes home. My Cardiff daughter, Dyfi had asked me if she could come to visit her mother with me that evening, and I was very glad she did.

THE ADJUTANT WINKED AT ME / *Carl Palmer*

Joan was not frightened of the operation, but I was apprehensive as I have always been frightened of hospital treatment. I was told to ring the ward at about 3.30pm and was informed that Joan was still in the recovery room, so that the visit should not be before 6.30 that evening. Enquiry as to how my wife was, resulted in the infuriating "as well as can be expected", so I held my tongue and longed for the evening.

I remember there was very little conversation as we walked into the hospital at just before six that evening. Joan was in a four bed ward, flushed and smilingly pleased to see us. She was sitting up with a saline drip up beside her bed and an epidural drip still in her back, she told us, for pain control. After gentle kisses from us both and minimal pleasantries, she told us they had taken a growth from her back, between her shoulder blades. The growth was on the Thymus gland and had been the size of an orange. If it had not been removed it would soon have grown large enough to cut off breath to the lungs resulting in immediate death. They had sent a sample biopsy to the path. lab, but would have no result until the weekend. Too stunned to speak, we both just stared at her. Guessing our feelings, Joan added with her unique smile, " The great news is, Mr. Corelli, the surgeon is certain he got all of it away. I didn't feel a thing, love, isn't that great?" Her face was bright, but her eyes were red-rimmed

Chapter 7 / PARTING, PROZAC AND PRAYERS

and I knew she was, to a large extent, performing for us.

Dyfi had brought clean clothes for her, and as I watched them talking together and holding hands, I knew that I mustn't show what I was thinking. We talked about our school days, Dyfi was now also a teacher, and I eventually told her how relieved I was at the fact that the operation was over, and how glad I was that this Mr. Corelli was so pleased at the result.

I will jump the three day interval filled with my apprehensions and repeated visits to the ward, as well as the fending off all non-family visits until we had the biopsy result. When we arrived on Friday evening, Joan was bright as ever, coiffed and fragrant as we stood at the bed end. "The tumour is called Thymoma", she said. "It was malignant. But Mr. Corelli said he was quite sure he got it all away. It's good news, kid" this last directly to me, as I stood quivering inside, but trying not to show it" I can come home on Monday." My heart lifted at this, but there was more.

"I've got an out-patient appointment at Velindre (cancer hospital) where they'll give me twelve radiotherapy treatments, then, he says, I'll be able to go back to work. Isn't that great, love?"

THE ADJUTANT WINKED AT ME / *Carl Palmer*

She came home on the Tuesday after her operation, white-faced, thinner, but strongly asserting Corelli's optimistic outlook for her. Within a month, she began the twelve treatments of radiotherapy as a day-patient at Velindre hospital which was about two miles from our home. The Head and staff in my school were very kind and I was able to ferry Joan to and from her treatments. She tolerated the treatment well, and the oncologist was pleased at the progress she made. 1988 dawned, and, by the Spring, Joan returned to work still with evident weight loss, but smiling at the prospect. I was worried at how she would cope in the classroom; she looked so fragile. For her it was a huge morale booster, and, to my great comfort she started eating better and putting on weight. I was hugely relieved and kept praying! In the summer we stayed in a friend's holiday chalet along the Pembrokeshire coast, just the two of us. We both benefitted by the rest and quiet. A new symptom had appeared: stabbing pains in the groin, so our walks were curtailed. We made an appointment for Joan to see our GP on returning to Cardiff and he was convinced that the pains were referred from the spinal radiotherapy treatment. She was prescribed pain-killers and we both returned to school in September.

At the end of the month, disaster struck. Joan's father died after a long degenerative disease at the age of eighty five. Joan, being an only child, was

Chapter 7 / PARTING, PROZAC AND PRAYERS

now saddled with the care of her mother. Although she was deeply upset, I noticed that Joan was not as upset as I had expected. Her dad had been ill for some time, so I assumed she was partly expecting it.

The programme of suffering for her had been continuous in any case. Because of her father's age the funeral was a small affair and her mother and she were not ashamed to say that they were glad the old boy suffered no more. Privately, Joan had confided that we would have to see more of her mother in the months ahead and I readily agreed.

I was teaching two weeks later when a colleague interrupted my lesson to tell me he would look after my class because the office had just heard from a neighbour of Joan's mother to say that she had entered her mother's flat to find a complete silence. She had walked into the bathroom to find her mother cold and dead in the bathroom. Apparently, Joan was crying uncontrollably and I was summoned urgently. When I got there, not many minutes later, I was alarmed at Joan's red and swollen face. She was crying hysterically and continued for the rest of the day. I must say, I sent up more than a few furious prayers to God asking him, why, why, why?

She recovered after a week, in time for the funeral which was exactly a month after her father's, but I saw a distinct change in her after that grievous

THE ADJUTANT WINKED AT ME / Carl Palmer

blow. The groin pains were now under control but had not gone away. As '89 started, Joan arranged her working week so that she always had Friday off, in this way she had a long weekend. It was towards the end of the year that I noticed a swelling on her back, underneath the scar tissue of her first operation. We were soon back at Velindre where a needle biopsy showed that the tumour was back. A further six radiotherapy treatments were prescribed after which the oncologist told us that the tumour had shrunk, but the groin pains were becoming severe, so, for the first time we were referred to the cancer treatment centre at Holme Tower. Here she was seen by the medical director who made it clear to both of us that the illness was terminal. Of course, we knew, but to have it stated was still a frightening experience. Neither of us looked at the other, for fear of what we would find, I suppose. The doctor told us that the palliative care Joan would now receive eliminated pain straightaway, so that a period of adjustment was now to take place requiring Joan to attend the Day centre on a regular basis. We left there feeling much happier than we had expected looking forward to Joan feeling better in the near future. I will never cease to be grateful to the doctor for that respite.

In early 1990, Joan decided to retire, finishing work in early March. Within a month, Joan told me at breakfast that she had difficulty in walking

Chapter 7 / PARTING, PROZAC AND PRAYERS

to the toilet in the night. Two nights later, she woke me with the news that she could not walk. We managed to get her downstairs on her bottom and, from there I carried her to the car and took her directly to Velindre hospital. I left her in a wheel chair because they told me that they would be doing tests and it would be best if I returned after school at teatime. In the late afternoon, I was in the hospital to be told by the doctor that Joan had been admitted, after a pause he added, "I'm sorry to tell you I don't think your wife will ever walk again."

During that endless stay on the ward, Joan endured great pain as she insisted that the physios did everything they could to try to make her legs work again. On morphine-based drugs, with their horrendous side effects she tried with a brave desperation to win against the dreadful disease. One effect of the drug was to make her hallucinate, so that to be with her for any length of time was to run the gauntlet of a rapidly changing mood pattern. Often she would snap at me with real venom, but I did not mind that if it helped her; my greatest torment, of being impotent to do anything to help her. All this suffering she endured, but her facial beauty never changed throughout the illness.

After Christmas 1990, Joan went into Holme Tower for assessment and the consequent adjustment of her drugs. Our youngest came home and announced that she wanted to get married to Adam whom she had been seeing for several years. Joan and I readily assented. Joan was glad for her beloved Catrin's sake, but she could not sit up, so this great occasion was the goad to a memorable act of bravery in my wife. She made enquiries of the medics at Rookwood as to whether it was possible to have surgery to her back which would enable her to sit up again. Glory be! the answer was ,"Yes!" Although the discs in her back had crumbled badly because of the radium treatment, there was a Chinese doctor who used a section of good bone from the pelvis to graft into the defective area of the spine which enabled patients to sit up again. This doctor warned my wife that it was high risk surgery. When Joan told me this, she laughed, "I should worry, eh love?"

The operation was performed in Cardiff Royal Infirmary at the beginning of 1991. I well remember my visit to her that evening after a wait lasting all day as she surfaced from the anaesthetic. She was swollen in her face and all over- barely recognizable, but she made it. All of us knew it was act of outstanding bravery. Six months later, radiant in a blue suit, she hosted Catrin's wedding in a marquee on a friend's land close to Cowbridge. In early August, wheel-chaired, but still very much her own woman, my wife became an in-patient at Holme Tower.

Chapter 7 / PARTING, PROZAC AND PRAYERS

Throughout the four and a half years of Joan's illness, Dyfi was a huge support. Catrin and Gareth lived in different parts of the country, so my older daughter, now with two daughters of her own, found herself solely responsible for visits to her mother in hospital and the consequent washing and ironing. She was all that a loving daughter could have been. She and Joan became very close as the cancer inexorably advanced. In the last stage of seven months at the Marie Curie centre at Holme Tower, I would go in to the early evening visit from six fifteen to seven fifteen pm and Dyfi would follow me in for the following hour; her contribution was indispensable to her mother and me. She never complained and was deeply involved in caring for Joan's plight.

In the following February with her family around her, Joan died. Her last words, the day before, spoken to the doctor about to sedate her with an injection were, as she looked around at the children and me, "It's all right for me," then pointing at us, "But what about them?"

Sister Mary Antonietta, the Head of the school where Joan taught spoke the eulogy at her funeral saying many kind and true things, but one sentence will always remain with me. Joan did not know God, but God loved her!" As she said this, the bright February sun flashed a heavenly endorsement through the chapel windows and I knew it was a message, "Safe home". Joan was such an honest person. She had that inner strength of an only child and had reared three children and developed an integrity widely admired. She was brave too, and this helped her to endure pain and suffering for years. She left this world more concerned for her family than herself. None of us knew just how much we would miss her.

I retired at 57, obtained a small enhancement of years served towards my teachers pension thanks to the NUT, and Invalidity benefit which enabled me to live comfortably and find something else to do with my life. Our parting was in February 92, and by July I had become a volunteer driver for Marie Curie Cancer Care taking cancer patients in to and home from the Day Centre at Holme Tower at Penarth.

That bereavement, if one ever recovers from it, is something I dread to relive. Parents die, friends die, close relatives die all causing that inexpressible pain that racks your body, and sobs which are agony to express. To lose your spouse, however is profoundly shocking. However you try to avoid it, the fact keeps coming back into your mind. "Never see again" repeating over and over and over, until despair is the only thing you can see. Then there is the calendar torment, when every day is "the day we

Chapter 7 / PARTING, PROZAC AND PRAYERS

went to..." The next stage is the hourly recriminations, "if only I had suggested ... Why I didn't try harder?"

Inevitably you are referred to psychiatry, which soon tries anti-depressants, in my case, Prozac. For the first few weeks you scoff at all the warnings you have heard about side effects. When the drug begins to make its presence felt you "suddenly" feel more optimistic ... your "old self" returns and in this way you are "better". For more than three years I took Prozac and as my mind recovered, I became aware that I had become someone else. Life seemed filtered through an almost opaque window, connection with reality became blurred. Then comes a desperate need to get off the drug, which was finally achieved at snails pace only under several supervisory visits to the doctor. In my case, it took nine months and the support of my faith to win the battle.

The activity of praying helps. In the simple shopping list one compiles to God, there is relief in the stocktaking of complaints. Ghost-like torments acquire flesh in this way and what you can see is much easier to deal with. perhaps the steepest mountain to climb is built of the sins acquired in the long period, nearly five years in my case, from diagnosis to departure (Notice, I still do not say "death" in Joan's case).

THE ADJUTANT WINKED AT ME / *Carl Palmer*

All my life at home with our family, I had been a consistent, but wobbly Christian, now, the wobble disappeared and I was able to appreciate the love of God which has always supported me and grows stronger by the hour. God has been good to me. You will agree that this book of my memoirs, gives more than a few examples of incidents where my escapes could well be attributed to divine providence. I believe with my whole mind that my survival has been due to just that: I thank God for it.

HOBSON'S CHOICE

As my life climbs up its eighth decade
The virtues I loved are extinct
This sad effect took not many years
But, happened one day when I blinked

The grass and trees have never been greener
As I walk out towards the world's shore
Enjoyment of life's simple things
Is keener than ever before

Getting up and breathing again
On a beautiful sunny morn
Prompt thankyous to your maker
For the day that you were born

But, on those rainy afternoons
When grey clouds crowd the sky
Your future shrinks to nothing
But the prospect of having to die

So, you draw up a balance sheet
Of things still precious at your age
The love of kin, good music, good food
Then, the plus points of quitting life's stage

Most of all, no more to be afraid
A bliss for which I've always yearned
Is achieved at last beyond the grave
Where meekness will never be spurned

No more to yield to temptations
Besetting sins you can't resist
Embarrassed to seek absolution
For confessionals do not exist

Death, the final analgesia
No need to conquer your pains
In tooth or in stomach or aching legs
Not even the memory remains

The rejection slip won't arrive again
Nor you'll never lose the race
Or hear you've been disqualified
For you have vanished without trace

Never again will they break bad news to you
That vacuum of being bereaved
Yours is the name in the black box now
You will never know how many grieved

Arms beyond the grave, your grandchildren
May only rarely bother to phone
Can only guess how much you loved them
Leaving them turns me to stone

The warmth of my semi in winter
Brands of dawn at the start of a day
Tears and smiles as I look at old photos
And the grave seems a long way away

No more to hear and see my children
Is something I can never volunteer
For although they will not believe it
Of life's blessings they were most dear

My life belt when seas have been stormy
Was always to trust in God's love
Now, the light waxing brightly before me
Assures me that heaven's above

So, at last I have come face to face
With God Almighty, Creator
"Oh it's you," he says as they usher me in
"Wait outside; I'll deal with you later!"

CEP June 2007

Epilogue

I am well aware that my frequent references to God in this book may have alienated people. In fact, I have been advised to reduce, if not exclude the mention of God or, risk the sale of my book. To ignore the influence of God in my life would be gross hypocrisy and appalling ingratitude. None of my friends would support the accusation that I am a "holier than thou" sort of person, nor would they describe me as a "goody-goody". I refer to Him often because it is to God that I attribute my ability to work as a Hospital Lay Chaplain approaching my mid-seventies, still busy after life has dealt me some disabling blows, in bereavement and bladder cancer.

The reader will remember that in an earlier chapter, my childhood conversion could be described as having dubious origins, which were bound to have caused wry smiles on the faces of the worldly-wise, but they will also remember the proverb "Great oaks ….." However, if my witness has made me a figure of fun, I enjoy the sound of laughter, and it will not make me hesitate for a moment as I go whistling on my way.

Acknowledgement

*To Susan, lawyer, lecturer, writer and friend,
whose knowledge of computer skills,
and authorship made the production of
this book possible.*

ISBN 142518139-2